THE
RED
CENTRE

H.H. Finlayson

Foreword by F. Wood Jones

ETT IMPRINT
Exile Bay

This 10th edition published by ETT Imprint, Exile Bay in 2023

First published by Angus & Robertson 1935. Reprinted 8 times.

Copyright © this edition ETT Imprint 2023

ETT IMPRINT
PO Box R1906

Royal Exchange NSW 1225 Australia

ISBN 978-1-922698-80-3 (paper)

ISBN 978-1-922698-81-0 (ebook)

Cover: The Red Centre

All internal photographs by H.H. Finlayson

Designed by Tom Thompson

to my Mother

Hedley Herbert Finlayson, in the Territory, 1936.
National Library of Australia.

CONTENTS

Foreword by F. Wood Jones 7

Preface by H.H. Finlayson 9

I.   THE LURITJA COUNTRY 10

II.   THE RANGES 16

III. THE "DESERT" 23

IV.   THE TORS 33

V.   ANIMAL LIFE 42

VI.   ANIMAL LIFE - Continued 51

VII. THE BLACK MAN 59

VIII. THE BLACK MAN - Continued 67

IX.   THE BLACK MAN - Continued 76

X.   CALOPRYMNUS 84

XI.   THE CAMEL 92

XII. THE CAMEL - Continued 102

XIII. THE CAR 108

XIV. THE WHITE MAN 117

Selection of Maps by Finlayson 129

The Musgrave Ranges and Ayers Rock 130

The Petermann Ranges 131

The James Range and Alice Springs 132

CREEK GUMS *(EUCALYPTUS ROSTRATA)*
In the Gorge of Stoke's Creek, George Gill Range; a fig scrub,
Ficus platypoda, against the cliffs.

FOREWORD

EVERY now and again we are told that some distinguished gentleman has arrived from overseas for the purpose of studying and collecting our interesting native fauna. And, judging by the Press accounts of these enterprises, we think very highly of them. Travelling facilities are generally placed at the disposal of the visitor. His description of the Nullarbor Plains, as he saw them from the Transcontinental train, is read with interest as being something of news value. His meeting with some station aborigines and his capture of a bandicoot provide the real outback atmosphere. On his return to civilization he is interviewed and he tells of his adventures in the great open plains. His specimens go to some museum overseas and everyone is satisfied.

And in all this we seem rather likely to overlook the fact that no fleeting visit to the Centre by a chance visitor can ever hope to reveal much of the realities of this vast region. Worse still, we are in danger of forgetting that in our midst there are some men to whom Central Australia and its flora and fauna are a hobby and a life study. For these men there are no waiting reporters, no travelling facilities offered by Governments. Their work is the work of love. Their quest is the quest of knowledge and the fruits of that quest are placed at the disposal of their country. They do not receive the adulation that we are accustomed to lavish upon distinguished visitors, but their work stands out as a great constructive effort amidst the destruction which is being wrought all over Australia by materialistic enterprises fatal to the preservation of the flora and fauna of the land. No living man has done so much in rescuing from oblivion those sparse but interesting mammals that still inhabit Central Australia, as has Finlayson. His rediscovery of the living *Oaloprymnus* was a romance of modern zoology.

The great John Gould had received three specimens from somewhere in South Australia in 1843. These three specimens in the British Museum remained unique. Oaloprymnus seemed to be as dead as the Dodo: and then Finlayson, with the assistance of Mr Reese of Appamunna, produced, as a conjurer from his hat, living specimens of the long lost Plain Rat-kangaroo. Finlayson has no story of thrilling dashes through the desert in high-powered cars: he has no delusions that his feet are treading where no white man's foot has trod before. But every word he tells is of the real thing - the Centre that he knows with familiarity; the animals of which he has practically a monopoly of knowledge; the natives, and that strange and undefinable attraction that the Dead Heart always has for those who have known the heat of its days and the cold of its nights - and the stars.

The average Australian knows very little about the Centre and unfortunately the information that is most readily available is sadly lacking in accuracy.

There have been many who have written of these things; but they have written after very varying experiences and apprenticeships. When Finlayson writes of the Centre and its fauna the reader may be well assured that he is reading reality - the reality of a man who knows these things with an unassuming familiarity.

F. Wood Jones

PREFACE

THE greater part of the material comprising the following chapters appeared during 1932-3 in the form of separate articles, and the suggestion that they should be given a more permanent form was due to Sir William Mitchell, K.C.M.G., Vice-Chancellor of the University of Adelaide, to whom I am greatly indebted for assistance and advice.

My cordial thanks are due also to Professor F. Wood Jones, F.R.S., who first read and criticized the manuscript in 1933, and later wrote the Foreword; and to Professor G.V. Portus for advice in matters connected with the production of the book.

I take this opportunity of expressing my appreciation of courtesies extended to me by the Surveyor-General of South Australia and his staff; by officials controlling the three Aboriginal Reserves of the central areas; and by others on the borders of the Reserves, who have furthered my work.

All photographs reproduced as illustrations are by the author, and all copyright in them is reserved.

H.H. FINLAYSON.
North Adelaide,
2 August 1935

1

THE LURITJA COUNTRY

THE naturalist in Australia who would study species in relation to their original environment, is confronted by extra- ordinary difficulties when he seeks an area in which the balance of nature may safely be supposed to be undisturbed and to represent the condition of things as they existed prior to European occupation. This is true to some extent of most groups of the animal kingdom - and of the plants as well; but it applies with particular force to the mammals, which bear the brunt of the attack at the very opening of the campaign of settlement, either pastoral, agricultural, or mining.

The initial stages in the opening up of the country may have been slow and full of difficulty, but the rapidity and relative completeness with which the tracks of the early explorers have been followed up by settlement of a sort is a striking and characteristic feature of Australian colonization. Once a way has been found and a technique of travel developed, the process of branching out from the original traverse proceeds apace and the whole continent west of the Great Divide now proves to have an accessibility by car, camel, and plane, undreamt of by our fathers and difficult to parallel in any other tract of similar magnitude in the world. The digger and prospector follow the explorer; the survey party follows both and makes record of their findings; and hard upon their heels has been the stockman with his cattle, horses, donkeys, and camels, his sheep and goats and dogs; and the great hosts of the uninvited also - the rabbits, the foxes, and the feral cats.

The results of all this are hailed by the statistician and economist as progress, and a net increase in the wealth of the country, but if the devastation which is worked to the flora and fauna could be assessed in terms of the value which future generations will put upon them, it might be found that our wool-clips, and beef and timber trades have been dearly bought.

True, much of the settlement so effected is very sparse so far as the human element is concerned, and incredulity is often expressed that such occupation as obtains in many parts of the interior, could have caused appreciable changes to the original conditions. It is not so much, however, that species are exterminated by the introduction of stock, though this has happened of ten enough, but the complex equilibrium which governs long-established floras and faunas is drastically disturbed or even demolished altogether. Some forms are favoured at the expense of others; habits are altered; distribution is modified, and much evidence of the past history of the life of the country slips suddenly into obscurity.

The old Australia is passing. The environment which moulded the most remarkable fauna in the world is beset on all sides by influences which are reducing it to a medley of semi-artificial environments, in which the original plan is lost and the final outcome of which no man may predict. From the point of view of the naturalist, the length to which the process of change will ultimately go is not to be measured by head of population per square mile, nor even by the numbers of stock which the country will carry, but rather by the presence or absence of sanctuaries where conditions are such that stock and all the disturbing factors of settlement cannot operate. One of the tragedies of this country is that it is almost destitute of such natural sanctuaries. There are no considerable mountain masses with climates sufficiently rigorous to discourage a stockman; few deserts or bad lands supporting any considerable fauna, which will not also support sheep and cattle; no great swamps and fenlands of a permanent kind; and but small areas where biological checks, in the form of parasites and diseases, form effective barriers to the introduction of domestic animals.

The man in the street has heard and read so much of a vast, empty centre that the conception of an untrodden wilderness enduring for all time has taken root. The extent of country which is listed in Commonwealth statistics as "unoccupied" - nearly forty per cent of the whole area - tends to support this idea. But it must always be remembered that even in those tracts where no stock have been depastured, those enterprising pests, the rabbits, foxes: and feral cats, have in many cases gone on before and worked untold change and damage.

The area which today presents the old-time environment unmodified is greatly reduced and is split into scattered portions. Of these by far the largest and (since it is being rapidly encroached on) the most important, is found in the western portions of the centre and comprises territory in the states of Western, South, and Central Australia. The westerly portion of this area is made up largely of sand-hill and spinifex country. It comes as close to the popular idea of a desert as anything which can be found in Australia, and, since it presents almost as small a range of animal life as it does of plants, it is of comparatively little interest to the biologist. But in the great Aboriginal Reserves, which lie on the intersection of the three boundaries, and also to the east and south-east of the Reserves, there is a country of fascinating variety in physical features, and with a comparatively wide range of vegetable and animal life, which, until quite recently, has suffered little disturbance of its primordial condition.

For lack of another name to distinguish this area from other parts of the Centre, I have called it here the Luritja Country, from the name which the Arunta blacks of the Macdonnells give to the "stranger" people, who, reaching the eastern limit of their wanderings here, extend far out into the western wastes to the fringe of the settlements in Western Australia.

The first work of discovery in the Luritja Country is due to Ernest Giles, who in the years 1872-6 led three expeditions into it with the object of forcing a passage across to the west coast. Until his return from Western Australia through Gibson's Desert in 1876 with camels, all Giles's work there had been with horses, and much of it had been carried on in the height of summer. All who have worked in that country since Giles's time have felt both admiration and astonishment at the splendid horsecraft, the endurance, and the unwavering determination with which those explorations were carried through. Men who have known the country over a series of years since then are inclined to believe that Giles was helped by very favourable seasons, as much of the area is now quite impracticable with horses. There is little in Giles's narrative to give colour to such a view; but even if the fullest allowances are made for this possibility, the discovery with the very scanty resources at his command, of the great system of ranges, including the Everard, Musgrave, Petermann, George Gill, and Rawlinson, and much of the country between, is one of the finest feats of exploration in the history of the Empire.

Following Giles's tracks fifty years later with camels and canteens, with maps and adequate supplies and friendly natives is easy, though not without its trials in summer; but the very advantage those facilities give brings home, as nothing else can, the crushing difficulty of the task he shouldered. To read Giles's simple account of those terrible rides into the unknown on dying horses, with an unrelieved diet of dried horse for weeks at a time, with the waters behind dried out and those ahead still to find, is to marvel at the character and strength of the motive which could hold a man constant in such a course. His work and that of Sturt, Eyre, and Stuart is a crushing rejoinder to those who see, or affect to see, no inspiration in the early history of this country, and no source of high tradition.

Giles's expeditions were largely financed from Melbourne through the enthusiasm of the botanist, Baron von Mueller. The rather large percentage of Teutonic place names bestowed by Giles on the natural features he discovered (a cause of frequent comment among bushmen), is due to the instructions of his patron. Petermann Creek, Mount Olga, Mount Liebig, Ehrenberg Range, Alfred and Marie Range, Schwerin Crescent, are a few of the many which are sprinkled over the map. The Victorian auspices: under which Giles worked apparently roused the jealous alarm of the South Australian Government of the day,

A SUNSET VIEW IN THE WARDULKA VALLEY, MUSGRAVE RANGES
Corkwoods, Hakea lorea, in foreground.

ERLIWUNYAAWUNYA
A famous rock-hole providing one of the chief waters of the Musgrave Ranges.

for, at the conclusion of his first short expedition, it dispatched two expeditions of its own to maintain its prestige. Both left the Alice; Warburton working north-west and Gosse, after an examination of the Western Macdonnells, turning to the south-west. Gosse followed Giles 's tracks down to Lake Amadeus and then, after discovering Ayers Rock, and being the first at Mount Olga, continued on south-west to the Mann and Tomkinson ranges, which he followed across the Western Australian border. His experiences contrast strangely with those of Giles, since he encountered frequent rains; and his movements were thereby facilitated to such an extent that his journey remains one of the speediest and most successful in the history of the early exploration of the Centre.

Following on these two contemporary pioneers has come a distinguished series of men who have filled in most of the gaps - so that today, so far as mapping traverses goes, it is better known than many other parts of the Centre. Zoologically, however, it is still largely unsurveyed. With the object of making collections of its mammals and of investigating their distribution, the writer made sojourns there in the summers of 1931-5 totalling thirteen months. In the chapters that follow an attempt has been made to give brief glimpses of its life and physical features.

To those who are interested in the original Australian environment the area makes a special and urgent appeal. In addition to its continued functioning as an Aboriginal Reserve, guarantees for its effective preservation for all time as a National Park should at once be sought, ere the rising tides of exploitation, work ruin on yet another of the wild places of the earth.

2

THE RANGES

OF the many misconceptions which find a place in the popular estimate of Central Australia, the idea of its flatness, of its treelessness and its monotony, is probably the most persistent. Even amongst those who have read widely in the literature of Australian exploration and have seen something of inland conditions, such impressions are often to be found. On reflection, it seems probable that the cause is twofold.

First, the frequent use of the word "desert" by some of the early explorers for all the country away from the ranges, has been adopted by some of the later geographers. No doubt the use of the word for an area of low rainfall and few surface waters is justified when applied to most of the interior; but it is most unfortunate that the popular idea of a desert is very different from the scientific one, and usually takes the form of a wind-tortured Sahara of drifting sand, whose chief function is to provide material for the "brickfielder" dust-storms which occasionally cloud the towns.

The second cause of misunderstanding arises from the fact that from all the settled areas of the south and east, the Centre must be approached through a belt of some hundreds of miles of pastoral country which, to a greater or less extent, has been wrecked by overstocking and other amenities of the white man's occupation. The traveller from Adelaide, for example, having cleared the Flinders Range, gazes out from the carriage window on the goat-made desolations which follow. He consults his time-table, and, finding that this change from the parklands has been wrought in four hundred miles, and that the Alice is still six hundred miles away, does some mental arithmetic, and concludes that Hades itself awaits him.

It is true that parts of the country, particularly of the Lake Eyre basin, come close even to the popular conception of a desert. But the Luritja Country - the south-west portion of Central Australia and 'contiguous tracts in the adjoining States - is totally different. Though the climate is rigorous, and the rarity of surface waters made the lot of the first-comers a hard one, the face of the country is varied, often attractive, and sometimes highly picturesque. The drabness which characterizes the more southerly dry country - the greys and dull greens, the fawns and faded browns of the saltbush tablelands, for example - have little place here; and it might well be known as the Red Centre. Sand, soil, and most of the rocks are a fiery cinnabar, and the grey mulga is liberally splashed with the clear green of ironwood and sterculia.

The country presents two very distinct environments - the ranges and the tracts surrounding them. First for consideration are the ranges, since from them the whole counry is naturally orientated, and the permanent waters which they hold are the pivotal points from which the country is worked over.

Judged by the standards of other lands or even of eastern Australia, they are but minor features. Few of them have a longitudinal extent of over a hundred and fifty miles, their breadth is usually less than fifty miles and their highest peaks rise no more than three thousand feet above the general country level. Yet in spite of their insignificant dimensions they are curiously impressive; and the first sight of a blue line of distant hills breaking the horizon of scrub is seldom without a pleasurable thrill. One enters their valleys as a refuge, for here is water and ease, and for a space one's eyes may rest upon sheltered scenes the nearness of which is a welcome relief from the vast prospects of the outside world.

They are bare, rocky chains, for the most part broken and weathered into wild and arresting contours; destitute outwardly of soils on their main ridges, timberless or with scattered cypress pines and mulgas, but supporting an interesting small flora in sheltered nooks and gorges.

Finest of all the Central ranges is the Musgrave. Although it appears to consist very largely of granite, the rock is fractured and altered over large areas, and the chain from the north or south presents contours totally different from those of the Everard, for example, which preserves the characteristic rounded, smooth bulges of the original granite intrusions. The southern front of the range is especially fine; one may ride for days along its foot with an everchanging panorama of jagged peaks and ridges, which never palls. From the far-famed Glen Ferdinand on this side issues the Ferdinand Creek, which, within a few miles of its exit, is joined by the Currie and other streams, together forming the Officer. The Officer is by far the largest channel in the Centre west of the Finke. For a hundred miles or more it sweeps on through the sandy country south of the range with an avenue of tall brilliant green gums fringing its wide bed. At fifty miles from the opening of the Glen, where it crosses a patch of spinifex and loose sand, it is still a hundred and fifty yards wide and with a clearly defined channel - a striking testimony to the immense volume of water which the range has shed at some former period of its history.

At Ernabella in Glen Ferdinand, the pioneers of the Musgrave have an outcamp which was my base for six weeks in a series of expeditions into the surrounding country over a radius of three hundred miles. The camp is in the heart of the hills and I left it, and came into it, from half a dozen different angles. After weeks in the scrub country outside the range, those home-comings to Ernabella are amongst the pleasantest recollections I have of the Centre. There seems to be no single vista round about it which lacks an element of striking beauty, or becomes com-monplace or dull. The peculiar feature of the Musgrave landscapes is the great development of grasslands. In amongst the hills, and frequently enclosed on all sides, and accessible only through rocky passes, are little plains of varying extent, and broad valleys, entirely free from bush growth, but with an even carpet of grasses and herbs.

The large open space of true "waving in the wind" sort of grass is a rare feature in this country of scrubs and thickets; and when they are backed by long vistas of blue hills falling away with a gently graded softening of outline into the distance, a combination is presented which stirs memories of a softer clime.

To Giles the Englishman - after weeks of bush-whacking in the mulga farther north - these views appealed with special force, and his descriptions of them are pathetically filled with a homesick longing which found expression in the nomenclature of the place. His maps are studded with glens and passes, tarns and vales. It must be admitted that Giles carried the matter rather far. Farther up the country some of his "vales" and "passes" are plains miles wide with scarcely a bump of any kind breaking the horizon. Twenty years after, Sir Baldwin Spencer was so disap-pointed with the Vale of Tempe that he was constrained to remark rather testily on the "ridiculous" character of Giles's names.

So far as they apply to the Musgraves, however, they are appropriate enough. Basedow, in the winter of 1903, was similarly impressed by the "unaustralian" character of many of its views - if one may put it so unpatriotically. Writing of Glen Ferdinand he states:

When the mists of evening rose and the light in the Glen grew dim, the blue-black thickets of mulga on the plain could no longer be distinguished from the pines on the hills, and I could scarce persuade myself to believe that the landscape before me was part of arid Central Australia, and not Thuringia or Tyrol.

I saw it all in the height of midsummer, when the green swards and wild flowers were no longer there to help the illusion, but even so the old-worldliness of the place was very evident.

Each range has special characters which give it an individuality of its own: the low rolling outline of the Everard, with its bare smooth domes and rock slides; the grassy pounds and conical peaks of the Musgrave; the extraordinary mural cliffs of the Petermann; the canyon-like gorges with their smooth rock basins which give the George Gill the finest waters in the Centre; and the glistening quartz screes that lie like a mantle of hail under the dark mulga, round about the Rawlinson.

THE SOUTHERN SCARP OF THE GEORGE GILL RANGE.

THE GHOST GUM *(EUCALYPTUS PAPANUS)*
A lunch camp near the Ruined Rampart in the Petermann Range.

When one reflects on them individually, these features come first to mind; but about them all there is the same curious atmosphere of aloofness from the surrounding country. They look out, as it were, over a world which has seen great changes, in which they have had no part. To walk alone into their gorges by moonlight; to look into the clear depths of their splendid pools when the noon sun flares on the rocks and the world is unbelievably still; or to listen to the dawn wind singing in the pines on their tops, brings always the same suggestion: a sense of things about them once familiar, but now long forgotten; a haunting nostalgia that will not be shaken off.

The feeling is stirred by many parts of the Centre, and is the secret of much of its rather melancholy appeal. It needs no foreknowledge of its geological history to see and to feel, for example, the influence of the old-time seas in shaping the contours of some of the lower lands. This impression of things anciently marine is especially strong about the George Gill Range. It rises as the scarp of an old plateau from a sandy mulga plain, which stretches away south two hundred miles to the Musgraves. It still retains its flat-topped outline, except where it is broken by steep little gorges and gullies, which, opening out suddenly on to the flats, are flanked east and west by bold crags and bluffs. As one rides west along the foot of the range, the feeling of something familiar about the whole scene recurs with tantalizing frequency. In the heat and glare of the sun the red rocks hold their secret well, but on the rare grey days when a fresh wind piles the clouds behind the hills, the changes of a million years fall suddenly away, and one remembers. Even as the light is fading, the mouths of the gorges have become little bays, the mouths of the gullies shingly coombs, and the crags and bluffs of the range are now the capes and headlands of a rocky coast-line streaming away into the west. "

Wondering at the transformation, one yet remembers the desiccation of the land. Surely no imagining could ever bring back to the thirsty sands the element whose waves would make the change complete - But as if to mock comes a vast whispering out of the south, and the stirring of those miles of usurping mulga is the very voice of the ancient sea, come into its own again.

STORM GATHERING IN THE PETERMANN HILLS
Mount Skeene in the middle distance.

3
THE "DESERT"

THE surrounding expanse, the tracts from which the ranges rise like reefs in a sea, are varied in character; but it is these that have chiefly earned for the Centre the stigma of desert from explorers and geographers. It has to be remembered, however, that the early explorers spent months in a state of tense anxiety owing to the complete uncertainty of water-supply; their recollections of the country were necessarily forced into a sombre mould by the constant struggle out of one "perish" into another. So if some of them subsequently wrote the country down, who shall blame them - A daily threat of death would spoil the charms of a paradise, and it is not pretended that any part of the Centre is that. As for the geographers with their statistics - well, all men know that figures, especially those with "damned dots" after them, can be made to prove anything. On the whole, there are so many redeeming features to offset the low rainfall and absence of surface waters, that a drastic restriction or redefinition of the word as applied to this part of the Centre seems long overdue.

Away from the ranges, the country might perhaps be broadly divided into three types-sand-hill belts, scrubs, and park-lands with the general interposition of wide transitional belts of intermediate character, particularly between the two latter. The sand-hill areas again may be subdivided into two kinds: small areas of knolls and hummocks and confused ridges, and much larger areas in which the ridges run parallel in fixed directions and are more or less evenly spaced by shallow swales. The axis of the ridges has been variously recorded, but though there is some variation, it would appear that in all larger areas it is about WNW.ESE., and is therefore nearly *parallel* to the direction of the prevailing wind and not at right angles as was formerly thought.

In the literature of the country, the sand-hill areas are usually referred to in terms of unmeasured opprobrium. They are certainly among the most difficult areas to traverse, owing to the conformation of the surface, the scarcity of the water and fodder plants, but they are by no means the bare and shifting dunes on which the popular idea of a treeless Centre is built. In most parts of the country they are fixed and permanent and vegetated; north of Lake Amadeus they carry dense forests of well-grown casuarinas forming very attractive and well-shaded landscapes, and south of the lake the swales separating them are loamy and carry kurrajongs, mallee, and mulga as well as the Ubiquitous spinifex.

In the parks and scrubs the soil is a sandy loam of varying firmness, and here again the surface is more often slightly undulating than flat. Indeed, strictly level featureless plains of more than a few acres are almost absent. A surprising feature of these zones is the variety and frequent density of the vegetation. Acacias, of course, make up the bulk of the medium-sized growth; colonies of the different kinds usually alternate with one another, and do not form many mixed communities. Chief amongst them are the true arborescent mulga (A. *aneura*), the staple camel-fodder of the country; the broad-leafed mulga or witchetty bush, the roots of which harbour a grub beloved by the blacks; and the little, narrow-leafed mulga of the sand¬hills.

The density of some of these mulga scrubs is very extraordinary in so dry an area: in the Allalgara and Erowa scrubs, and in parts of the country between the Everard and Musgrave ranges, and south of the Rawlinson, the "sticks" are so densely packed as to form almost impenetrable thickets. It is in the occasional clearings of these dense patches that the mound-building *Leipoa* has her nest, and the mallee hen of the south becomes a mulga hen in the Centre.

In this virgin country the mulga, both in its bushy and arborescent forms, is an attractive symmetrical plant, very different from the tortured, twisted remnants which survive the persecution of stock in the occupied areas. Like most plants of the Centre, it blooms after any heavy rain, apparently largely independent of the season of the year. The flower is a little golden-yellow bottle-brush, deliciously scented, and when a rain-storm has raised new life in hundreds of square miles of mulga parks, the expanse of blossom and its perfume are things not easily forgotten. At the present day one would not associate the town of Oodnadatta with the romantic appeal of a perfumed flower; but those who have supposed that the place was named by Afghan and Baluchi camel-drivers may be interested to know that the word is a perfectly good aboriginal one for the mulga bloom.

On the fringes of the mulga colonies, or running as belts through them along the shallow watercourses, are a score or more of large shrubs or small trees - some rather unfortunately named in popular usage and subject to much confusion of identity; water-bush, turpentine bush, corkwoods, needlewoods, beefwoods, mallees, myalls, gidgees, quondong, plum-bush, whitewood, etc.

Of the larger trees of the sand areas, undoubtedly the most characteristic is the desert oak, the finest of all the casuarinas. It grows to a height of forty feet or more, usually in open groves destitute of any other growth save spinifex. In a melancholy way it is a most beautiful tree with dark drooping plumes of "foliage" and a stem which appears jet black against the bare red sand.

In varying degrees, the bulk of the larger vegetation shares that reproach, so often laid upon the Australian foliage by visitors, of being a dull grey or brown-green-to the new-comer depressingly different from the cheerful bright woodland greens of the northern lands. But in the Centre this applies chiefly to the bush or shrub growth; and amongst the larger trees are at least four species which, in the brightness of their foliage and roundness of their contours, at times do much to provide a welcome contrast. First and most beautiful is the ironwood (A. estrophiolata), widely spread over all the sand country, sometimes in the form of open parks, sometimes in little groups of five to ten trees. The leaf is small and narrow but the foliage is profuse, and the tree has a rounded compact top which throws the densest shade to be got in the Centre. After long intervals of drought its colours may fade till it is as grey as the mulga; but it responds with extraordinary rapidity to even trifling accessions of moisture, and after rains, or when it can tap underground supplies, its foliage is a brilliant lush green, rivalling a new-dressed English oak in freshness. Less widely distributed, but welcome for the same reasons, are the sand-hill poplars (rather aptly named) and the kurrajong, which, south of the Mann and Tomkinson, forms forests of considerable extent, periodically visited by the blacks, who garner the rich oily seeds.

Of the big eucalypts, the creek gums in the gorges and main channels have a much brighter foliage than their congeners farther south and perhaps the most beautiful picture of the Central vegetation one may see, is of the dainty ghost gums, with chalk-white stems gleaming in the slanting light of a late afternoon, their brilliant green tops thrown into strong relief against the red cliffs. The ghost gums are the very antithesis of the desert oaks.

Of the hosts of smaller plants, the so-called saltbush, bluebush, cotton-bush and buckbush, are at all times the objects of a good deal of attention, since it is to them that one looks chiefly for horse-feed and a change from the top feed for the camels. They are small shrubs, rarely exceed-. ing two feet in height, widely spread over the more open parts of the country. The true saltbush (*Atriplex vesicarium*), the most nutritious and valuable of them, is unfortunately less common than farther south, but a larger relative, (*Atriplex nummularia*), forms extensive colonies, particularly along the north side of the Musgraves.

Quantitatively the buckbush (*Salsola kali*) is the most important of this group. It is a short-lived plant which appears in extraordinary profusion after heavy rains, and plays a leading part in those beautiful transformations which occur at such times, by covering wide areas of otherwise bare sand with a luxuriant mantle of light green. It goes,

THE GIANT SPINIFEX (TRIODIA ARISTATA); MUSGRAVE RANGES.

MULGA GRASS IN THE MUSGRAVE RANGES
Showing the characteristic spirally twisted habit of the tussocks in summer.
Water-bush, *Grevillia nematophylla*, and Mulga *Acacia aneura*, left foreground.

however, as quickly as it comes and after a week or two of hot dry weather it dies off, and, being then extremely brittle and shallow rooted, is easily blown away and pulverized, leaving little in its place save a carpet of prickly seeds.

The grasses, though less important than the salsolae, are nevertheless well represented, especially in the areas around and within the granite ranges. The mulga-grass (*Anthistiria sp.*), one of the best fodder grasses, is conspicuous in summer owing to the curious spirally twisted habit assumed by the tussocks during desiccation; the outer layers of dry stems uniting at the top to form a little tent which protects the still green base from the sun. One of the most interesting of the grasses, however, is not touched by stock. It grows chiefly in the rocks and is remarkable for its delicious rose-geranium scent. It is, in fact, an Andropogon species (*A. exultatus*), closely allied to the aromatic grasses from which in India, Ceylon, and Java the fragrant essential oils of citronella and palmarosa are distilled.

For the rest, one can only refer to the sprightly purple and yellow flowered succulents, the parakeelia and munye-roo, and to the porcupine grass. Surely this so-called "spinifex," the *Triodia* of botanists, is the most maligned of all Australian plants. In the journals of almost all the explorers its name is coupled with such adjectives as horrible, beastly, devilish, and useless, so that one might think it a plant with no redeeming features at all. But this is far from the truth. Of the several species, some of the lower ones, in which the-annular type of growth around a dying centre prevails, are uninspiring; but in the granite country of the Musgraves there is a magnificent species which forms huge hemispherical mounds as high as a man and twenty feet in diameter. The flowering stalks are yellow and the plant is massed so densely on some of the slopes of the hills, that they appear like fields of giant corn. The seeding tops of most species are excellent fattening feed, and to the student of mammals the plant is always of interest as it determines quite definitely the distribution of some of the most interesting herbivorous mammals of the Centre.

The area under consideration lies between the tropic of Capricorn and latitude 28° 30' S. Its climate, in brief, is one of very hot dry summers and moderately cold dry winters. Though the economic disabilities of this aridity may be crushing, in matters of personal comfort it is a great advantage and one's energy output under extremes of temperature is much greater here than in more humid and (from the economist's point of view) more favoured districts, where the thermal range is much less.

It is enclosed by the eight-inch rainfall line of most of the existing meteorological maps; but the records are too sparse as yet to make possible a reliable estimate of the average annual fall, which is highly erratic and derived largely from very local storms. Rains, though more frequent perhaps in the summer months, may occur at all times of the year. The northern edge of the tract, including the Rawlinson and northern part of the Petermann Range, appears to lie just within the influence of the southern monsoon, and though this influence is weak and irregular, these hills and, in less degree, the high ranges farther south, are somewhat better favoured than the rest of the country, where the average fall is probably not more than five inches per annum.

Though the rains are incalculable and capricious, imposing demonstrations which delude one with an immediate promise of rain occur in the late summer with considerable regularity. The morning sky during the hot weather is brilliantly clear, but from January to March, noon frequently brings a gathering of clouds. First come tiny white patches low down on the horizon. Then fleets of silver canoes float up all round the rim, and, coalescing, are suddenly transformed into fat shining wool-bales. Slowly these grow bigger and mount higher and grow darker until in mid-afternoon they reach the zenith to fuse and form a continuous pall that suddenly shuts out the sun.

Almost invariably the threat is an empty one, and after a period of silence and expectancy, the whole spectacle goes into reverse. The curtain splits up into detached masses, the sun breaks through, and within two hours the last trace of cloud has melted away, leaving the sky clear and hard as in the morning. One gets so accustomed to these empty threats that the rare occasions of a consummation are doubly impressive; for storms result, such as we never see nor hear in the south. I was caught in a series of them when travelling alone with two camels near the Mural Crescent in the West Australian Reserve and the effect upon the camels was not the least disturbing part of the experience. On each occasion the pall formed overhead and a stillness fell, as I have described. Plodding on through the gloom one came to listen with a certain dread for the signal - most uneasy of sounds-which never failed to usher in the debacle - the distant moaning of an approaching wind when all about one is still. When the storm broke, the uproar was as though the hills were being torn to pieces; and the rain, if one may call it that, fell in sheets, blotting out detail in the scrub a hundred feet away. On the last occasion of this series of storms (14 February 1934), the rain began at 6 p.m. and continued till 11 p.m., and within thirty minutes of the first drop the whole country-side near the range, sandy as it was, was covered with a sheet of water four inches deep, flowing swiftly towards the lower country. Feeling the sand liquefying under their feet, the camels (always distrustful of false footing) became terrified. They cried and whimpered like children and floundered wildly about so that I was hard pushed to get them to a gravelly knoll in time to prevent them throwing their loads into the mud, which for two days after the storm effectually prevented any travelling.

An interesting meteorological phenomenon of the Centre is the frequent occurrence in summer of fogs. They have been scarcely mentioned by most writers on the country, being usually dismissed under the term haze, which gives one little idea of their real nature. They are frequently so dense as to blot out the outline of massive objects at three hundred yards and render travelling in broken country a hazardous proceeding. All well-marked occurrences that I have personal knowledge of followed periods of strong east wind; the thickest developed on the second day after the storm described above, the first day having been calm and perfectly clear. Somewhat similar effects have been recorded in the southern portions of the Sahara, where they have been attributed to heavy distant rains and the simultaneous presence in the air of fine colloidal clay dust.

The seasons, though well marked by temperature changes, are not emphasized by synchronized changes in the vegetation, as they are farther north and farther south, since rapid growth, blooming and seeding of plants, take place after any sufficiently heavy rain, largely independent of the time of year.

All who have experience of the winter months in the Centre have spoken well of its bright, bracing days (if somewhat less enthusiastically of its freezing nights and mornings). It is the long rigorous summer, however, which, in popular estimation dominates the weather of the Centre; and the descriptions of Sturt, Eyre, and Stuart have given such an impression of a hell of heat that incredulity is often expressed that anyone should go willingly into it. True, the noonday heat and glare sometimes attain a pitch of intensity which demands for its enduring an almost conscious physical struggle; and such weather as prevailed in January of 1932, when shade temperatures ranging from 122 degrees to 125 degrees were recorded, and birds and beasts died in thousands, is not to be recommended to those who are unaccustomed to high temperatures or who set great store by their ease.

There are compensations, however, to the ordeal of the middle hours, and they have not been given much prominence. The diurnal temperature change in the high areas of the Luritja Country is marked and fairly constant; in thirteen summer months I cannot remember more than three evenings which were uncomfortably warm in the open. The Musgraves particularly, rising at Mount Woodroffe to nearly five thousand feet, have evening mists and fresh mornings even in January; indeed in all parts of the country the early mornings from daylight to 8 a.m. are delightful. So totally different are those few easy hours of coolness and soft light from the strain of the growing heat, that later in the day, when the sun has taken full charge, the events of the early morning seem curiously remote, and things which happened two or three afternoons ago, seem nearer in time than those of daybreak.

But even when the heat is at its worst and a certain peevishness is apt to tinge one's outlook, one cannot escape a realization of the magnificence of the flood of radiant energy that beats upon the land. In retrospect, it is not the passing discomfort of the temperature that comes to mind, but rather a vision of great red landscapes, wide open to the splendour of the sun.

AYERS ROCK
Looking west down the north face; the camels in the left
foreground are about four hundred yards from the base.

4

THE TORS

THE ranges are not the only features which break the uniformity of the lower country. There are salt lakes varying in extent from a few acres to vast expanses like Lake Amadeus; there are stony tablelands; and there are isolated rock outcrops ranging from the little granite" jump ups" round about the Everard and Musgrave, to huge tors a thousand feet high.

Of the tors, the most notable are Ayers Rock, Mount Olga, and Mount Conner. These afford sights which are among the most remarkable of the whole continent, and Ayers Rock more particularly, may fairly be claimed as one of the most wonderful natural features in the world.

Ayers Rock and Mount Olga, which are only twenty miles apart, lie roughly half-way between the George Gill and the Musgrave ranges, with Mount Conner about sixty miles to the east of them. Mount Olga was named by Ernest Giles from a distance on his first expedition of 1872, but he was unable to get up to it because Lake Amadeus, which lay between, was at that time impassable for horses. A few months later W. C. Gosse, coming south from the George Gill a little to the east of Giles's tracks, saw and named Ayers Rock and Mount Conner, which had been missed by Giles; and he was the first white man to visit and describe the more westerly pair.

The approach to these latter, by way of King's Creek in the George Gill Range, is the traditional route of the blacks to whom Oolra and Kuttatuta, as they call them, are objects of considerable occult significance. This is also the route adopted and described by Sir Baldwin Spencer during the Horn Expedition. At the time of my visit to the George Gill, with B. Bowman of Tempe, it was impracticable with horses; but later I was able to make the journey with camels from the Basedow Range, a hundred miles east of the rock.

The party consisted of W. Mackinnon of the Commonwealth Police, who was on his way out to the Petermann on patrol, W. H. Liddle, the pioneer settler of the Basedow Range area, and myself. We got away under very favourable auspices after a splendid four-inch rain, with a string of twelve camels and two "boys." After clearing the end of the Basedow we headed a little south of west and plodded on from sunup to sundown, as one's way is with camels, doing two to three miles an hour through an open mulga park. From occasional sandstone rises there were fine views of Mount Conner to the south-east but the Rock was lost in the fine haze. From Carmichael's Crag in the George Gill Range, on a clear day, one may see both Ayers Rock and Mount Olga, though they are nearly a hundred miles distant. But coming in from the east it was not until the third day, when within about forty miles, that the Rock could be made out with certainty: a low ovoid shape, pale purple, and scarcely differentiated from its background of pale sky.

The mulga stretches away west in a splendid dark green undulating sea, and the only topographical incident of note in the first two days' travel was that most pleasing of discoveries in Central Australiaan unexpected water: a series of clay-pans freshly filled by the recent rain and now gleaming still and yellow in the hot sunshine. Though the expanse of some of these clay-pans is considerable, sometimes many acres, the supply they afford is very transient, owing to their shallowness and the extraordinarily high rate of evaporation. The water is held up by a thin layer of excessively fine colloidal clay resting on a bed of sand; and bitter is the disappointment of those who attempt to dig soaks in the pans when the water is gone, for the clay while wet is so impervious that scarcely any percolation of water takes place, and at a depth of a few inches the sand is likely to be as dry as it was before the pan filled.

While it lasts, however, the milky clay-impregnated water is deliciously sweet, and few can find it in their hearts to pass so gracious a gift of the gods, whatever their preoccupations may be. With a light heart we emptied our canteens of the brackish water we had brought from the hills and in refilling them through improvised filters of towels and handkerchiefs the swarming life of the tepid water was forced upon one's notice. There are water-beetles of several kinds and tiny molluscs, but that which takes one's eye, and never fails of interest, is the crustacean *Apus*. Rather like a little king crab in appearance, with a round green-and-brown carapace about the size of a shilling, and a tapering tail of an inch or more, it gathers in serried ranks round the margins of the pools. Here it lives out its brief life of a few days in a feverish search for food, and yet more food, to the end that it may reach maturity, and complete its reproductive cycle before the water, which gave it life, finally disappears.

As the pans dry, the water recedes towards the centre, and *Apus* follows the tide until at last a seething mass of millions is concentrated in a shallow puddle. And now the insectivores amongst the birds and beasts become for the moment cancrivores and even the wild dog does not disdain the feast spread out on the fast-drying mud. But though she meets a tragic end, *Apus* does her duty to the race right well, and the clay in all the bigger pans is now liberally seeded with ova. When the next rain comes, another generation springs suddenly to life, if other conditions are suitable, and the brief drama is played over again.

On the third day, the mulga comes to an end, and we enter a belt of sand-hills which extends for thirty miles and to within two miles of the Rock. Although fairly well vegetated and by no means as desolate as the spinifex type of ridge, they are, nevertheless, exceedingly monotonous. For twelve hours we toiled over them in seemingly endless succession, the crests becoming steeper and the troughs narrower as we advanced. The Rock is now in plain sight and becoming redder and redder with every mile; and Lake Amadeus, though we do not sight it, is only ten miles north at one stage and makes its presence felt by a damp, salty breeze from the north-west which recurs at intervals all day. The proximity of the two great rocks to the salt lake has impressed the imagination of the natives. Liddle, who is well versed in such matters, relieves the tedium of the day with lively accounts of aboriginal legends, touching the origin of all three. Simple, curious tales, meet for venerable anthropologists, but far too curious, far too simple, I fear, for the general reader.

When we topped the last sand-hill the sun had just set, and the Rock was suddenly before us. But the crowning impression of that long day of approach was not to be of the Rock itself, amazing as that feature now revealed itself to be.

Away beyond it in the west, clear against the evening sky, but with its outlines softened by twenty miles of distance, was Mount Olga. In the finished symmetry of its domes it is beautiful at all times; but now the sunset works upon it a miracle of colour, and it glows a luminous blue against an orange field, like some great mosque lit up from within. Five times I saw the sun set beyond. Mount Olga, but in five hundred times it would not pall. It is the most delicate sight in all the land. We watched it while the light lasted; then moved in nearer, and camped half a mile from the Rock.

In the morning we embarked on the fascinating business of examining and photographing it. No descriptions I have read adequately prepare one for the simple grandeur of the thing and its impressiveness. It is usually described as rising sheer from a sand plain, but it would be more correct I think to say that it occupies the centre of a shallow oblong basin with a diameter of four to five miles, distinctly below the average level of the surrounding country, and possibly formed by the scouring of centuries of winds round the base of the mass. In approaching it from the north, the east, and west, it is not until one is within two miles of it that the full dimensions of the thing and its proportions can be fully grasped.

The Rock is one and three-fifths of a mile long from east to west, seven-eighths of a mile wide and eleven hundred feet high. It rises abruptly from the sand with sides that are nearly vertical, even in some parts overhanging slightly, and the impression of vast height is augmented by the total absence of any foot-hills or skirting outcrops, or even any considerable accumulations of weathered debris. Its outline is a smooth unbroken ovoid, and the greater part of its surface is also smooth, even

CHAMBERS PILLAR
A residual sandstone pillar amongst sand-hills on the Finke River.

CYLINDRICAL ROCK SHELTER NEAR THE BASE OF AYERS ROCK
West side.

polished. But, on the north face particularly, some weathering has gone on and has produced deep pot-holes in the rock and some roughened patches having a striate lath-and-plaster sort of texture, and grotesque shapes. The largest of the patches can be made out at a great distance, and is somewhat like the sagittal section of a human skull, with mandible attached.

The exfoliate type of weathering characteristic of granites, in which the surface layers of the rock spring away from the main body, forming thin plates, owing to strain set up by rapid temperature changes, is also to be observed, though apparently it is proceeding very slowly. To this disruptive agency, however, must be attributed a very curious feature at the north-west corner. It is a huge curved pillar or slab perhaps two hundred feet high, which, though it appears to be welded to the main mass both top and bottom, is nevertheless quite separate from it in a considerable part of its length, so that when viewed from the side a long narrow slit of daylight can be seen between it and the parent rock.

At close quarters it can be seen that the Rock is marked with vertical striae, especially on the lateral buttresses of the north side, which at first sight appear as bedding planes vertically tilted, but which in reality are drainage lines of water, which, after rains, seeps down from the natural reservoirs on the top. Few white men have seen it during thunder-storms; but those few have seen a sight which is surely one of the strangest in the world. Gosse witnessed it, and refers to it briefly in his journal, but I have had a first-hand account of it from Allan Breadon, one of the most experienced of Central Australian bushmen, who visited the place in the early eighties and saw the Rock during heavy rains.

The physical phenomena which attend the sudden precipitation of huge volumes of water down semi-vertical non-absorbent slopes may no doubt be stated prosaically enough in terms of hydraulics, but to appreciate the visual and auditory effects of a storm at Ayers Rock, with its weird anomalies of sudden deafening sounds rending the stillness, and of white cataracts of foam eight hundred feet high veiling the red sun-baked walls, one must have some background of experience of the place itself. Truly it is a country of contrasts, but few so staggering as that.

The aggregate capacity of the basins on the top and possibly in the interior must be immense, since, long after the rains, the internal seepage serves to keep three magnificent pools on the north, west, and south sides constantly replenished during months of dry weather, when the prevailing temperature, and the rate of evaporation, are both excessively great. The pool on the south is fed by a particularly copious drainage, which has come to be known as Maggie's Spring, though it cannot be relied on as a permanent water.

Near the base are numerous caves. The lower ones take the form rather of overhanging cylindrical rock shelters, whose long axes are parallel to the face of the rock. These are frequent resorts of the wandering Luritjas, as the paintings on the walls attest, and in them are stored dried bundles of the native tobacco (which they chew as a narcotic) and of another poisonous plant, *Duboisia hoowoodi* - a camel poison of the whites - with which the blacks poison the smaller rock-holes, so that the water-greedy emus become stupefied and fall easy victims to the spear.

Higher up, the caves take the form of deep clefts running far back into the mass. These are not used by the blacks but are tenanted by rock wallabies, opossums, bats, and rodents. I spent some time in examining their tracks on the floor of a very large cave on the north side, a hundred feet or so above the base, and it was on emerging late one afternoon that I first noticed that all the world to the east as far as the eye could reach was divided into two moieties by a dark band. In that open country, where the sun meets few obstacles higher or denser than a mulga, it comes as something of a shock to realize that the dark band is the shadow of the rock towering a thousand feet above the floor of the cave.

Everything about it is huge; but it is not this alone which makes it so impressive, nor even this added to its utter unexpectedness, its isolation, and its brilliant red uniform coloration. Underlying and reinforcing all these impressions is a sense of the oneness of the Rock - its purely monolithic character. It is without seam or cleavage; a great pebble, as truly integral as the smallest that one might pluck from a river-bed.

During our first day there Mackinnon decided to attempt to scale it. It is a difficult climb and only four white men before him have succeeded, the ascent being made at the only practicable point, which is on the west side, where a buttress slopes down at a rather gentler grade than elsewhere. As my time was now short, Liddle and I were forced to leave him, with his boy, to win his alpine laurels, while we pushed on for Mount Olga. But we learned subsequently that he had triumphed, and, the day being very calm, had reached the top in forty minutes. The more or less flattened top of the Rock is a jumble of lightning scarred hillocks and basins. Vegetation, completely absent from the sides, has succeeded in establishing itself on the top, and both mulga and biack wattle are fairly plentiful. It is an isolated botanical experimental station ready made.

The sun was low when we reached the foot-hills of Mount Olga. Coming to it from the east, slowly mile by mile, there is a certain disappointment in its aspect. The whole thing flattens out and the symmetrical globes, which twenty miles away at sunset seemed to rise unsupported from the sky-line, are now seen to emerge from a rather prosaic jumble of foot-hills three or four miles long and two miles deep.

But on rounding the south-west corner, the whole vertical western face of the mass comes suddenly into view with a shock for which the eastern approach leaves one quite unprepared. Five huge bluffs, 1400 feet high, separated by vertical ravines, and accurately aligned from north to south, stand guard over the western plain. Each bluff is a single towering rock and it is as though a higher and longer Ayers Rock had been slashed into five blocks by great vertical cuts extending from the top to the very base. The summits of the bluffs are rounded into domes, and it is these which, by rising far above the eastern foot-hills, form the majestic outline of a mosque which distinguishes it in a distant view.

Like Ayers Rock, it is coloured a brilliant red, but whereas the former is a conglomerate so fine in the grain that it might easily be taken for a granite, Mount Olga is composed of pudding stone so constituent particles vary in size from a motor car to a walnut, In spite of this, however, its outlines and surfaces are as smooth as, or smoother than, those of the Rock, and, though it shows both vertical drainage lines and horizontal bedding planes, it has not undergone the pot-hole or exfoliate type of weathering of the latter.

The occurrence of these two isolated conglomerate masses, while to the north of them are chiefly sandstones and to the south quartzites and granites, cannot fail to awaken curiosity even in those whose interests have few geological leanings. Dr Charles Chewings, who adds to his theoretical knowledge the advantage of long residence in the Centre, tells me that the debris, which by consolidation has formed both features, was derived from great ranges to the south-west, which have now been entirely denuded from the face of the land. But there are apparently still many gaps in their geological story to fill in.

Whatever their past history may be, the two great rocks in their present aspect, may well stand as symbols of the land itself: huge; red; bizarre.

MOUNT OLGA
General view from the west.

5

ANIMAL LIFE

THOUGH animal life is varied and sometimes plentiful, it is remarkably unobtrusive, owing to the large proportion of forms that are strictly nocturnal and burrowing in habit. During the day, one may ride for hours at a time and see no living thing, except the inevitable ants and flies; and but for the tell-tale sand, one might conclude, as some of the first comers did, that there was nothing else there to see. But at night the bush comes to life, and the tracks tell a story which the blacks read, literally as they run; and even the dull white man, if he sharpen his wits by studying their methods, may thereby feel the pulse of the country.

One must say inevitable, in speaking of ants and flies, because it is sad but true, that in summer at any rate, there are few occasions when they are not painfully in evidence, and at times they become an intolerable scourge.

The species of ants are legion and their numbers as the sands of the sea. The kind that inflicts most misery on the traveller is a small black *Camponotus* which, though almost ubiquitous, especially favours certain types of sparsely vegetated loam flats. It concentrates also on certain trees, such as the ironwood, whose welcome shade one always accepts with some trepidation on that account. Some of the loam flats are closely reticulated by its tracks – "ant roads" as the camel-boys call them – where for miles it would be unsafe to kneel a camel down to adjust a load. This little ant is abroad during the whole twenty-four hours; but it is chiefly at night that it is to be dreaded, and a camp in "ant country" leaves a painful memory. To lie down is to be immediately infested with them and, though their bite is not severe, the incessant crawling over the skin is a torture which, as Giles relates in his account of the Rawlinson, can only be escaped by walking about all night.

The fly has only to be endured by day, and the nuisance it causes can be mitigated somewhat by the use of nets, but in the absence of these it is a greater affliction than the ants. The prevailing species, *Musca vetustissima*, concentrates in enormous swarms in the lush new vegetation which springs up after flood rains. It is no more than half the bulk of the common house-fly, *Musca domestica*, but much more aggressive and persistent in habit, and is not to be frightened away by a wave of the hand, but must be brushed from the skin. A gastric disorder, known to the settlers by the crude but expressive term "barcoo spews" is common in summer, and its spread is often attributed by them, not improbably, to the prevalence of this fly.

Heavy rains stimulate other forms of insect life less chastening to man. In the Musgraves in December 1933, after a series of falls which ran the Ferdinand Creek, there was witnessed one of the most fascinating of entomological spectacles – the swarming and metamorphosis of a cicada on a grand scale.

The species involved was *Thopa colorata*, which in the familiar adult condition is seldom seen in large numbers in this part of the country. In the larval form it dwells underground in deep burrows of its own making, where it lives by sucking the sap from tree-roots. The period of its larval life is uncertain and perhaps variable; it must sometimes extend to many years, for although the blacks have a name for the creature, few of the younger men I questioned in the Musgraves had ever seen the winged insect. The larva is a rather forbidding looking, more or less beetle-like creature about three-quarters of an inch long and of a dull brown colour. When it feels the urge to enter upon its new life it crawls briskly out of its burrow and ascends the nearest gum-trunk to a height of four to five feet. Here it selects a favourable spot, anchors itself firmly to the bark by means of its powerfully hooked forelegs and then becomes perfectly immobile-and as far as its larval life is concerned, "dies." Within a few minutes of its "death," however, its horny case splits open down the back and the adult form of the creature slowly emerges, becoming quite free in about half an hour, and ranges itself alongside the empty case.

The newly emerged insect is an exquisite thing of very pale smoke-grey, with large transparent wings delicately patterned in green. It is an inch and a half long, with a wing-span of four inches, and a more astonishing contrast to the ugly gnome-like larva, it would be difficult to conceive. It remains quite stationary on the bark, while the wings slowly unfold and harden, and at the same time it begins to change colour, till at the end of an hour, it is a rich red-brown with splashes of scarlet on the sides and jet-black crescentic markings on the thorax. With wings now hard and serviceable, the cicada launches itself on its first flight which takes it no farther than the top of the nearest and most suitable gum-tree. Here, in the fierce sunlight of the upper world, the males begin their terrific song; a song which has induced modern Americans to bestow upon them the elegant name, "screech bugs," and which inspired a Greek of old to a cynical couplet which has been quoted by most writers on the cicada in the form:

"Happy the cicadas' lives,

For they all have voiceless wives!"

How many millions were singing in the trees I will not venture to guess, but the numbers involved in the transformations were enormous; not only the trunks of the creek gums, but much of the smaller vegetation as well, was smothered with larvae and their empty cases. The noise was tremendous and all pervading. When it ceased for a moment, the relief was like the lifting of a burden. It went on day and night for a week or more, with occasional brief intermissions as though some warning signal had spread throughout the multitude. The noise is somewhat suggestive of the "revving" of an electric motor, 'and has the same short-pulsing quality: imitated by the Luritja name for the cicada – tcheereeree.

The life-span of the adult insect is not accurately known, but apparently it is limited to a few days, during which the female lays some hundred of eggs, in crevices of the bark. From the eggs small larvae subsequently hatch, and these crawl down the trees and burrow into the soil to wax great by sap sucking, and prepare themselves for the call which, years hence it may be, will take them to the tree-tops.

The birds, diurnal and active as they usually are, contribute much less to the interest of one's travelling than they do farther south, since they are more dependent on water than any other section of the fauna, and several species, such as the splendid scarlet-tailed black cockatoo, the rose-breasted galah and the smaller hawks, seem scarcely to leave it during the daylight. Their presence in the timber lining a creek-bed may generally be hailed with relief as indicating the presence of surface water, which, even if one is in no immediate need of it, is never without interest in a droughty land.

The massing of the bird life about the waterholes provides some of the most astonishing sights of the country, both by reason of the incredible numbers of some species and the extraordinary displays of colour which result. The two species seen most, the shell parrot or budgerigar, and the chestnut-eared finch, occur literally in millions, and the latter in particular provides the aborigine with his standard of numerical vastness. If you inquire of a buck whether kangaroos are plentiful in his country, he may tell you either of two stories. If he does not want to be bothered, and thinks that you are going to ask him to come with you, he will say (if he has any English) that they are "done finish altogether long time;" but if he wants meat and thinks you will get it for him, he will encourage you by saying that the 'roos "sit down like a mob of waxbills;" from which you conclude, having gathered wisdom, that if you walk all morning you may get two or three shots.

Early morning is bird-time *par excellence*. In those few cool hours most gregarious species seem to take the air for exercise and play, and the parrots, especially, are more in evidence then than at any other time. Of the budgerigars one never tires. Round the waters they manoeuvre in gigantic flocks, to be measured in acres, rather than thousands of birds, and as they wheel and turn, alight and take off again, with synchronized precision, they make a flashing spectacle of brilliant green in the early sunlight.

KOORACARDIE
The sand goanna (Approximately one-fifteenth natural size).

YALLARA
A rarer rabbit bandicoot, *Thalcomys minor miselius,* allied to the talgoo.

To a very large extent it is a land of lizards. In summer these are practically the only terrestrial vertebrates seen at all frequently during the heat of the day. They are of great variety, and many of the smaller kinds are brilliantly coloured or quaintly shaped, like the tcharcoora, the spiny *Moloch horridus*, and the long-legged barking gecko. Of the larger kinds, two species of monitors, the goannas of bush lore, are more often seen than any others, and scarcely a day goes by without encounters of some sort with these two great lizards, on account of the blacks' fondness for them as an article of diet. The smaller is the kooracardie (*Varanus gouldii*) a beautifully coloured lizard with a delicate lace-like pattern of purplish-brown on a pale yellow field; the larger is the nyntucka (*Varanus giganteus*), apparently specifically identical with the better known parentie, farther east.

The nyntucka is rather ornamental, too, having a pattern of transverse rows of yellow spots on a black ground, but is chiefly remarkable for the huge size it attains. Easily the largest lizard in Australia, it is possibly second only to the Varanus of Kommodo Island, in all the world of lizards. There are few authentic records of its size and weight, but specimens eight feet long, weighing twenty pounds, are occasionally taken; and judging by skeletons unearthed in old tchungoo warrens, the animal must on occasion greatly exceed that bulk.

Many tales have been told of its ferocious character; of gins being badly mauled and lacerated and of legs being broken by blows of the beast's tail. That is has the strength and armament to inflict such damage there is no doubt; but the estimates of its ferocity and aggressiveness are greatly exaggerated. I have seen dozens killed by the blacks and in no case has there been the slightest show. of resistance. When approached, it generally stands its ground, but more from stupidity than courage, and if the first stick thrown misses, it makes for the nearest rocks or warrens. The biggest specimen I have seen was killed by a boy and girl of fourteen who went about the job with the greatest nonchalance and armed with sticks which they plucked from a dry mulga.

When cooked *a la* Luritja, in the ashes, the white flesh of both species is very tasty, although the supposed resemblance to fish is remote. The great attraction of the goanna to the aborigine, however, is not the flesh but the fat, which is nearly always present as two long fillets lining the belly on either side. In a land where mammals are nearly always lean, the big lizards and the emu are practically the only sources of fat-supply and are cherished accordingly. Having killed his goanna, the black man, or black girl as it more often is, proceeds to examine the condition of the prize by pinching the belly; if the luscious deposit is not up to specification, it is very often consigned to the bush again. But it is a poor day when two or three kooracardies or nyntuckas are not swinging from the saddles by sundown.

Of the snakes, the best known are perhaps two large pythons, the endoorema of the rocks and kunea of the sand-hills. These are taken without hesitation and eaten, but for many of the smaller species, whether venemous or not, the blacks have a lively dread. It is interesting to find that exaggerated or mistaken ideas about the lethal qualities of reptiles are just as prevalent amongst them as with our own people. For example, the comical little barking gecko (*Nephurus laevis*), which shares the burrows of the native mice or mingaries, and which is perfectly harmless in spite of the bold front it offers to an intruder, they regard with horror and will on no account touch.

The mammals of the area are so obscure in their ways of life, and, except for a few species, so strictly nocturnal, as to be almost spectral, but in spite of this unobtrusiveness it is about them that much of the interest of the life of the Centre gathers.

They are of interest on purely mundane grounds because they form the mainstay of the black man's diet and make important contributions to that of the travelling white man too. It is remarkable how, after a week or so of damper and tea, persons who ordinarily have little leaning towards mammalogy, will develop a keen and even anxious interest in that study; and will inquire plaintively of their blacks regarding the possibility of augmenting the pot with a tasty tchungoo, a tender if grotesquely shaped talgoo, or even, *in extremis,* the greasy, insectivorous and therefore weirdly smelling, wintarro.

But for more abstract reasons they claim attention, because although of all the animal groups they are the most distinctively Australian – the farthest sundered from their allies in the great world outside-yet in the Centre it is amongst the mammals, that one finds perhaps most clearly those specializations of structure and habit, called forth by increasingly arid conditions, which echo, if only feebly, the specializations of the perfected desert mammals of the Old World. One must say feebly, however, because the changes in the fauna, as one moves from the coast to the Centre, are by no means commensurate with those differences of climate and vegetation which sunder the two zones so strangely. And in the Luritja Country, while there are a few forms exclusively adapted to a Central Australian Environment, there are many more which are closely related to, some actually identical with, those which live in a sixty-inch rainfall in the coastal belts.

Around these facts centre some of the most interesting problems of Australian natural history. They demand for their solution more data than is at present available, and perhaps more than we shall now ever obtain. But it may be said that the evidence of the mammals goes to show that, if the more pessimistic of the geographers are right, and the Centre is a desert, then at least it is the veriest newcomer amongst deserts, and many of its denizens retain with charming conservatism, habits which have obviously been developed under much less rigorous conditions of climate than now obtain.

From the general rule of a strong preference for night life, there are only three exceptions amongst the mammals; the red kangaroo, the euro, and the rock-wallaby. On ordinary occasions when one rides, walks, or climbs abroad, these are the only species likely to be seen in broad daylight.

The kangaroo, or merloo as the Luritjas call him, is the familiar red kangaroo (Mocropus rufus) of the saltbush tablelands farther south, and he is not only the finest of Australian mammals, but one of the handsomest in the world. The race which inhabits the Central areas, how-

49

ever, is smaller and paler than in the south; and the does, in place of the familiar, delicate, slate-blue coloration usual in the saltbush belts, are more often pale tan like the bucks. Moreover, the virtual absence of open plains in that area of the Centre under consideration, has forced it to adapt itself to a life in mulga scrubs, and this again has reacted unfavourably on its gregarious instinct, so that now it tends to be rather solitary and lives usually in pairs or in very small parties. After thunder-storms have revivified the grass, the merloos, guided to the spot by some uncanny and never failing instinct, concentrate upon it with a swiftness which passes belief, and they may then be seen in large numbers, but the big "mobs" which are familiar sights in many parts of the pastoral country farther south are not ordinarily seen, and constant hunting by the blacks keeps them wary and suspicious.

The lower slopes of the ranges are the stations of the short-limbed, broad-chested, sturdy, hill kangaroos or euros (*Macropus robustus*). And on the craggy tops, where eaves and clefts in the weathered rocks afford them shelter, are the beautiful silky coated rock-wallabies (*Petrogale lateralis*) whose sprightly acrobatics amongst the boulders may have given rise on the east coast to an early report that monkeys were to be found in Australia. The euro or kunala, is a brilliantly coloured animal, the adult males having a short coarse shining coat of a rich, red-brown above, with pure white chest and throat. Though it belongs to the same species as the well-known black wallaroo of the Great Divide of the eastern States, it is a very different animal in appearance and in order to find a nearer ally one must travel over spinifex and sand, six camel weeks to the north-west, where the red hills of the Kimberleys reproduce the conditions of the Central ranges.

6

ANIMAL LIFE (Continued)

THE kangaroo, the euro, the rock-wallaby, and the emu, are the big game, the red meat, of the lords of the land, who take little active interest in small fry. Upon their gins devolves the constant task of digging out the smaller mammals to supplement the larder, and from them a wealth of material and data may be obtained which is otherwise most difficult of access.

Remarkable amongst the smaller forms is the talgoo, one of the so-called rabbit bandicoots, which has carried a number of structural peculiarities to grotesque lengths yet manages to reconcile them all in a surprisingly harmonious, and even beautiful, whole. A large male weighs as much as four pounds. The head tapers rapidly to a long-pointed snout and the ears, which are narrow, are five inches long and so thin and flexible as to have almost the texture of oiled silk. The tail, about ten inches long, is jet black for about half its length, then changes suddenly to white and terminates in a pure-white silky crest, much sought after by the natives for ornamental purposes. The coat is one of the most beautiful amongst the marsupials: fine, silky, slate-blue, and quite like chinchilla. But the general aspect of the animal recalls a miniature aardvark and it resembles that African animal in being a most powerful burrower. The talgoo is largely insectivorous; in parts of the country thousands of acres of loamy mulga flats have been closely harrowed by its scratchings in search of beetle larvae, which occur there.

Two other bandicoots, the walillya and the wintarro, are widely spread, and make similar scratch holes in search of insects. And amongst the insectivores, also, must be numbered the little pitchi-pitehi (*Antechinomys spenceri*), of interest because it is unique in the zoophagus group of the marsupials in hopping like the kangaroos instead of running

NILEE
A little carnivorous marsupial, *Sminthopsis crassicaudata cent alis*.

THE MAALA DRIVE

like all its nearest allies. Excessively slim and with greatly elongated hind legs, it has come to bear a remarkable resemblance to the so-called kangaroo-mice, which, in enormously greater numbers, share its habitat.

The marsupial mole, which the blacks call eecharricharri, affords the best illustration of a mammal exclusively adapted to an arid sandy environment, and not found elsewhere in Australia. The "mole," although widely spread, is rarely seen, since it is only in dull weather and after rain that the upper world seems to have much attraction for it, and the rest of its time is spent in driving shallow tunnels through the sand in search of the insect larvae which form its diet. The blacks delight to point out to one its brilliant metallic coat and shovel-like hands and in laughing pantomime will imitate its swimming-like action as it breasts through the surface sand. Its adaptations to a sightless, burrowing life have made it so astonishingly unlike any other Australian form, and so like some of the moles, that its marsupial character was at one stage called in question.

In the Centre, as in most parts of the Australian region, truly carnivorous mammals form a very small and obscure minority, both as to the number of species and of individuals. The western "native cat" (*Dasyurus geoffroyi*), with his coat of pure-white spots on a fawn ground, is there, but nowhere common; and there are several species of pouched-mice which are at least occasional flesh eaters. But the most interesting and most plentiful of the carnivores is the mooritja (*Chaetocercus cristicauda*), known to many Western Australian bushmen by the ludicrous name, "Canning's little dog," in allusion to the large canine teeth which are always bared. Old males are occasionally taken as large as a brown rat, but generally it is considerably smaller. Rather like the native cats in build and physiognomy, it can at once be distinguished by the curious vertical crest of jet-black hairs which stand up from the surface of the tail like a zebra's mane. It is the boldest and most ferocious little beast in the country, and, having a passion for fat, will raid the camp fearlessly if it can obtain so rare a delicacy. Ordinarily, however, its mainstay is the native rodents, and woe to the sluggard who leaves rattraps uninspected over night, for in the morning, if the mooritja has been abroad, he will find only empty skins.

There is a widespread idea amongst Australians that all the "native" animals are marsupials. But nowhere in the country can that opinion be proved more fallacious than in the Centre, where true indigenous rodents vastly predominate numerically over the marsupials, and even in point of species and genera, make a brave show in the list. Most attractive, certainly most plentiful, are the beautiful soft-coated kangaroo-mice of the genus *Notomqe*, already referred to, which the Luritjas call dargawarras, They average about twice the bulk of a house mouse but are built on totally different lines; with elongated hind limbs, very short forelimbs, long ears and a long, bushy tail. When undisturbed and feeding quietly, they go on all fours, but when startled, they take to their hind toes and bound like tiny kangaroos. The legs are so thin that when moving rapidly they are almost invisible, and the thing has rather the appearance of a ball of down being blown along, rather than an animal under its own motive power.

The dargawarras and most of the smaller rodents are largely committed to a diet of seeds. Although they rouse the ire of the settlers in the pastoral country by destroying melon plants and such, in the little patches of garden which the gins maintain near the wells, they are not herbivorous to any degree. This fact is evidently responsible for some curious anomalies in distribution, for whereas heavy rains and the resulting increase in green feed and insect life usually result in a large increase of true herbivorous and insectivorous forms, the smaller rodents and the mooritja which preys upon them, frequently disappear from the favoured areas at such times, and there can be little doubt that the sudden diminution of the seed-supply by germination, or possibly its removal by the surface wash, is the chief cause. It is, of course, not only the mammals which are affected by the change. Many species of birds, and some species of ants, probably react to the deprivation more promptly than the rodents, and in general these fluctuations in the seed-supply may cause far wider repercussions in the fauna than one suspects;

the influx of herbivorous forms, which is an obvious consequence of most rains, being accompanied perhaps by an unsuspected exodus of seed-eaters.

Of the smaller herbivorous marsupials, two of the most interesting are the hare wallabies known as the maala (*Lagorchestes hirsutus*) and the oqualpi (*L. conspicillatus*). The latter is a northern form, which in the central areas does not come much south or west of the Macdonnells, while the maala, though common in the more westerly spinifex tracts, is not often taken east of the Reserves. In 1932, requiring fresh specimens of *hirsutus* for comparisons with the newly rediscovered *Caloprymnus* from the Diamantina, I spent much time in likely places where it was reputed to occur, with the main object of getting it, but without success. A year later, coming down from Oparinna to Erliwunyawunya on the south side of the Musgraves, we learned from the blacks that there was a small colony of maalas in a spinifex patch ten miles south of Koonapandi. It was a long way from the nearest water, but too good a chance to pass, so leaving my companion with most of the string at Erliwunyawunya, I went on down with four camels, taking along three of the bucks and two "weeis;" bright boys of about fourteen.

The patch of spinifex was about ten square miles and surrounded by dense mulga. We made it in the late after-noon, "uished" the camels down under a splendid solitary ironwood, and carefully planted the boxes and the precious canteens in its shade. In the canteens we had exactly thirty-four gallons of water; and all who have experience of the enormous appetite and capacity of the black man for the ever necessary "karpee," will understand something of the anxiety with which I endeavoured to make all hands "hold off" the water, so that we could stay out long enough to get what I had come for. The black man's spirit may be willing, but his flesh, in matters of appetite, is woefully weak, and I was hard pushed to arrange matters so that none of the five were ever in camp alone with the canteens.

A preliminary survey of the ground before the light went showed the presence of maala tracks in plenty. The maala lives almost exclusively in these pure spinifex communities, feeding upon the spines, upon which it thrives exceedingly and grows fat, and finding shelter in small, perfectly protected squats under the arching pincushions or in small burrows leading down for a foot or two from the same. The blacks' favourite method of taking the animal is to fire the country, but if the wind is unsuitable, he does the second best thing, which is to follow the freshest tracks to a squat and then, while two or three stand ready with throwing-sticks, another jumps upon the tussock and breaking down the shelter, sometimes exposes the maala, which has no time to use the burrow. The spinifex hereabouts is a large sort with spines like a darning-needle, the points of which easily penetrate the uppers of one's boots; yet the blacks jump into the clumps without the slightest hesitation, and beyond rubbing their calves afterwards with the edge of their wommeras, I never saw one show any signs of discomfort.

The first two days were calm, and the second method having yielded no results, hope began to dwindle almost as fast as the water. But the third day was ideal, a scorcher with a hot north-west wind. As we left camp in the early morning for the ground, the blacks were in great spirits, chanting a little song to themselves, twirling their fire-sticks and at intervals giving instructions to the two weeis, who had not seen a maala drive before.

On leaving Koonapandi the bucks had made no secret of the fact that they were maala experts, and the doings of that day fully bore them out, for event followed event to a final success, with the precision of a ritual. The whole procedure adopted appears to have become standardized and perfected by age-long repetitions. Firstly, runners are sent into the wind with fire-sticks. They diverge from the starting-point along two lines, and, thrusting the torch into spinifex clumps at intervals of about fifty yards, they soon have an open horseshoe of flame eating into the resinous and almost explosively inflammable vegetation. The extent of country fired depends, of course, on the size of the party operating, but in the present case when the runners were recalled, the arms of the horseshoe were nearly two miles long and the extremities at the open end which faces the wind, were nearly a mile apart. The country outside the horseshoe is left to its fate, but matters are so arranged that the areas where maala tracks are thickest are within the lines of flame, and upon this space attention is focused.

The subsequent events form three distinct phases, during each of which some kills are made. The fire, of course, makes rather slow headway against the wind, but as it creeps on, all life forsakes the tussocks well in advance of the flame and a steady concentration of all living things is effected. As the flames advance into the wind, the party recedes from them slowly, keenly watching for a breakaway from every likely looking tussock, and should a maala break cover within range, his chance of dodging the throwing-sticks is slender. This is the first phase, and it occupied most of the morning. But while this has been going on the extremities of the wings of flame have been closing in and when at last they meet, the action suddenly quickens and the second phase is ushered in.

With the wind full behind it, the closed line of flame now rushes back towards the starting-point, and to the steady roar of the leeward fire is added the sudden menacing boom of the windward one, changing from time to time to a crash, as some isolated patch of mulga or corkwood is engulfed, and swept out of existence in a second. The party now gathers up the spoils already taken and dashes through the leeward fire to the safety of the burnt ground beyond, and there, in line, await the meeting of the double wall of flame, when every living thing which has remained above ground must come within range of their throw.

It is a time of most stirring appeal. The world seems full of flame and smoke and huge sounds; and though the heat is terrific, yet one is scarcely conscious of it. In the few tense moments that remain before they break into frenzied action and frenzied sound, I watch the line of blacks. The boys can scarcely control their movements in their excitement; the three men, muscled like greyhounds, are breathing short and quick; they swing their weight from foot to foot, twirling their throwing-sticks in their palms, and as they scan the advancing flames their great eyes glow and sparkle as the climax of the day draws near. It is their sport, their spectacle, and their meat-getting, all in one; and in it they taste a simple intensity of joy which is beyond the range of our feeling.

It is soon over, and we go back to the ironwood camp in mid-afternoon to wait for the ground to cool before beginning on the third and final phase. It might be thought that such a fire would wipe out every living thing in its path, but that this is by no means so, can be seen from inspection of the ground afterwards, when fresh mammal tracks are in plenty; it follows also from the fact that the whole business has been carried out systematically for untold generations and over enormous areas of country. At such times the burrowing habit is the salvation of both mammals and reptiles; and as there is no massive smouldering debris as in a forest fire, it is only a matter of a few hours before most forms are on the move again, looking for pastures new. But the prickly vegetation having been swept away, the sites of the burrows are exposed and the subsequent digging operations much facilitated. The maala, which makes only a shallow pop hole, now falls an easy victim.

Following up the third phase carried us over into the fourth day. When we got under way for Koonapandi, the canteens were empty and dry, the water-bag empty and dry, and we ourselves empty and very very dry, as we had averaged less than six quarts a day per man since leaving the hills.

But in my saddle-bags was a very satisfactory series of *Lagorchestes hirsutus*.

7

THE BLACK MAN

REGARD him as you will, the blackfellow* bulks large in the affairs of the Centre. He may be to you a companion and an indispensable aid to your work; or he may be merely an object of anthropological interest. You may find in him many of the qualities of character and personality that make for reciprocal friendship; or you may find no more than a complex of appetites and reactions, not very different from that which prompts the behaviour of any other of the predatory carnivores, which share his habitat. He may rouse your interest to a kindling sympathy with his problems; or you may turn from him in disgust. But if you remain long in his country you cannot be indifferent to him, since almost every activity of a white man there depends ultimately for its success on the blackfellow's co-operation.

The word Luritja, as already mentioned, is an Arunta one, meaning "stranger," and though the term is now also used in a more restricted sense for a group of people in the Western Macdonnell and James ranges, who are the immediate western neighbours of the Aruntas, it is here employed in a general way for all the" desert" people who extend west of the Larapinta Country, over a vast territory, reaching almost to the Western Australian coastal belts. In that part of this area now under consideration, the bulk of the aboriginal population speak of themselves as Pitchenturras. Other names are used to distinguish other

* The absence from the literature of the subject and from general usage, of any name to comprehend the whole of the indigenous Australian people, is an embarrassment which leads to the adoption of such terms as this, which, however uncouth, are generally understood without ambiguity. A simple name, preferably derived from their own tongues, is much needed however. Over large portions of the interior the aborigine distinguishes himself from the white man by the term "waddi" and this might perhaps serve as a name for the race.

small groups; but all appear to be racially homogeneous, and speak with little modification a common Wongapitcha tongue.

They lead an almost perfectly nomadic hunting life, and their wanderings are conditioned almost entirely by seasonal factors in the life-histories of the animals and plants which make up their food-supply. They form no permanent camps, and except on the infrequent occasions of important corroborees, or when widespread shortage If water effects a concentration, they are distributed over the country in small bands or groups of families, which rarely exceed twenty or thirty souls. In proportion to the huge area they occupy, they are but a handful; but their mode of life makes any reliable estimate of their numbers a matter of difficulty.

In physique, the typical western desert black is a fine figure of a man. Though he tends to be sparse, this, in a good season, is by no means carried to the point of emaciation; the thin, calfless legs, which have been held to detract so much from the appearance of the blacks generally, are by no means the rule here. It may be noted, however, that this condition is not necessarily a defect in physique in the sense that it implies a failure in adaptation to the special mode of life adopted. Many men of middle-age are as heavily muscled about the upper parts as the average white man. In emergency they are capable of extraordinary feats of endurance in covering long distances in a short time and without sustenance; but ordinarily their ability to endure heat and thirst and hunger is not notably greater than that of a white man accustomed to a hazardous and vigorous life.

In the matter of food and water their appetites are gigantic, and the quantities of both which they will consume are almost incredible. I have seen two men eat a large kangaroo, at least fifty pounds of meat, at a sitting which lasted from noon till dusk; and on another occasion an emu was polished off by one man in three sittings. This voracity extends to children as well, and boys of twelve or fourteen will eat twice as much meat and bread at a meal as a hearty white man, and whatever degree of repletion is reached, to refuse food is almost unheard of.

In the course of their travelling, the blacks of necessity frequently abstain from drinking for stretches of many hours, and in doing so seem to suffer, or, at any rate, show, much less discomfort than a white man would under the same test; but when the opportunity comes of slaking their thirst, they perform feats of swilling far beyond any white man's capacity. There are few reliable records of the actual volume of water they imbibe on such occasions, but one well authenticated instance, comes to mind of an old man acting as a shepherd, who, at the end of a long hot day's work, went straight to a clay-pan and drank a steady series of seventeen "jampeters," which, when measured, worked out at just over three gallons. It is unfair, however, to set down these enormous consumptions of food and water as gluttony. An ability to ingest huge quantities of both at such times as they are available is probably a valuable accomplishment, and a necessary factor in nutrition under a scheme of things where no provision is made for the preservation of food, and its provenance is subject to great irregularity.

They are perhaps less distressed by the extremes of summer heat than most white men, but the differences are not great; they are reluctant to travel in the hottest weather, and when forced to do so, take every available shade which offers.

I had a good illustration of this once in going up to Oparinna, in the north-western spurs of the Musgraves. There are corroboree grounds of great sanctity near the springs, and two of the older men were detailed off to "show us the way." The way was obvious enough, as the place is approached by a valley which rapidly narrows to a gorge. But that was their polite way of putting it; actually the two ancients were there to see that we did not by inadvertence trespass on any holy ground. We started at about 10 a.m. on a day of stupefying heat. At the beginning, the bucks strode manfully enough, one at the head and one at the tail of the string, and they did the honours by reversing their spears and exclaiming with hospitable and reassuring smiles, "karpee eela" (water close up), but actually it was eleven miles away, nearly four hours with the camels, and the two blacks soon showed signs of distress. The heat in the gorge was terrific, and in spite of the rubber-like calloused pads on the soles of their feet (up to a quarter of an inch thick) the burning sand was too much for them, and the nearly vertical sun compelled them to shield their heads with bunches of mulga twigs. After three miles, they deserted their posts and progressed in a series of desperate rushes from shade to shade. Arriving at a mulga, they would sit down gingerly on their sunshades, and nurse their feet until the camels were abreast of them, when they would rush to the next tree, and so on. Panting like dogs and drooping pathetically, they would not accept our offer of mounts, but battled on still smiling and still pointing the way to karpee.

For several reasons, it is not usual for these people to camp in the immediate vicinity of waterholes; but in the height of the hot weather, if sufficient game is to be had near by, they sometimes concentrate on the larger holes to indulge a taste for water sports. At such times an unwonted holiday spirit seems to pervade the camp, and the long day through the water is thronged with a miscellaneous but happy assemblage of men, women, children of all sizes, dogs, and possibly the camels of a passer by. Both men and women swim freely, but the proceedings are mostly confined to the shallows where scenes of uproarious hilarity are enacted, with much good-humoured horse-play of duckings and mock drownings, splashing and wrestling and a constant babble of shouting and laughter. The water, of course, under these conditions, rapidly acquires considerable body, but the domestic supply is obtained by sinking little soaks round the margins of the pool.

When game is plentiful in a restricted locality they may "sit down" for several weeks and they then build wurlies. These are of the flimsiest description, albeit skilfully and expeditiously put together, and serve well enough. But when the rains catch them on the move, they suffer severely, as they are very sensitive both to cold and wet.

An interesting example of their reactions to such conditions occurred in the summer of 1932. We were camped near a party of about twenty blacks on an open loamy scrub flat, when, with very little warning, a rain came on which developed into a four-inch fall. It began in the early evening and rained incessantly all night, with a gusty wind, until 10 a.m.

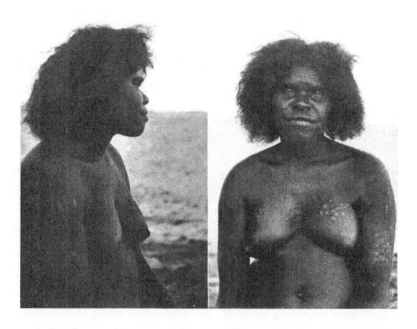

A WOMAN OF ABOUT THIRTY YEARS, PETERMANN RANGES

THE USE OF THE SPEAR
An Everard Ranges man with *kudgee* and *meru*.

next day. With the aid of our ground-sheets we managed to keep ourselves and most of our belongings pretty dry, though we passed a miserable night, but I shall never forget the sight the blacks presented next morning, when it was light enough to see. At the onset of the storm they had crawled under the witchetty bushes, and by interlacing the foliage with the stems, had made partial breaks against the wind, but of protection from the rain they had absolutely none. They were huddled together in groups of three and four, the women crouched on all fours to protect their youngest children, who were under them, and the men in sitting posture, with their heads bowed between their knees, and their hands clasped on their necks. The water poured from their glistening black skins, and at each gust of wind they shivered so violently that they could scarcely maintain their position. Yet in some miraculous way they had kept their fire-sticks going all that night, and when the first break came, they were all out paddling in the surrounding ankle-deep sea looking for kindling; in half an hour they had a great fire going on a little rocky rise and were fast regaining both circulation and cheerfulness.

Amazement has often been expressed that the aborigines make no use of hides in constructing coverings to mitigate these discomforts, and the fact has been regarded as another instance of their "lowliness" and "stupidity," and "sluggishness." No-one, however, who has seen the combination of acute observation and deduction, with boundless energy of application, which they bring to the solution of their hunting-problems, could subscribe to that idea. The explanation lies, rather, in a deep-rooted dislike they have for all impedimenta when on the move. They will tolerate no sacrifice of mobility. A hunting party may decide suddenly to move on to another ground. Without more ado, the men reach for their spears and walk away, and their women follow, carrying no more than a yam-stick, a uiirra, and their youngest child. The journeys thus casually begun may amount to hundreds of miles and extend into weeks of walking; and they must find their food and water as they go. Under such conditions of life, can it be wondered at that they have elected to put up with the occasional discomfort of the rains rather than the constant discomfort of burdens - After all, in evolving a capacity to endure, they have acquired something much more portable than a skin tent or a fur cloak.

It is difficult for us, whose lives are deep rooted in a sedentary habit, to realize that their normal state is an ambulant one. From the settler's point of view it is a valuable trait, as there is never any difficulty in obtaining messengers for even the longest journeys. Not only do they enjoy the constant change of scene, but they are flattered by the deference shown to envoys, and take a pride in getting through. In the bad old days of early settlement undesirable bucks were got rid of by giving them "paper yabbers" to deliver to distant neighbours. The note would read, "Keep this b - moving," and he would immediately be sent on to the next man, and so on, until after months of travelling he would find himself stranded, perhaps in a hostile country, hundreds of miles from his own territory.

Normally, neither sex wears covering of any kind. The Government, however, requires all settlers who employ blacks in stock work, to provide clothes for them, and some ludicrous situations result. Most of the' camel-boys employed by the whites wear trousers and boots, which they come to regard with considerable pride, as a sort of insignia of office in the eyes of their less sophisticated brethren; the utility of the garments being quite a secondary consideration. In spite of their heavy pigmentation and the matted shock of hair which covers the head in the men, it is noticeable that most of them are decidedly intolerant of a vertical summer sun; quite as much so, I believe, as most white men. I have often noticed in travelling that, as noon approached, the trousers were taken off and the legs tied round the owners' neck, so that the seat hung down over his shoulders as a cape, or could be brought up over the back of the head as a sunshade. If the prickles are not bad, the boots also are often worn dangling round the neck. When W. H. Liddle first issued clothes to his shepherdesses, they accepted them with glee, but valued them far too much to wear them long. It was their custom to leave the camp in the morning wearing the clothes, but when a mile 01' so out they would remove them, and r eturn in the evening with them rolled up as a bundle under their arms. Ultimately all the clothes were cut up to make pituri and tea and sugar bags.

Unfortunately this attitude which is characteristic of the uncontaminated myalls gives place in the more settled country to a great liking for clothes. The change is a most unfortunate one in every way. So long as he is quite naked he has a natural dignity of bearing, and is comparatively clean, but when he dons the cast-offs of his white master he becomes a pitiful scarecrow. Moreover, since he knows nothing of those instinctive precautions against accumulating filth which long ages of experience in the wearing of clothes have taught the white man, he rapidly becomes foul and verminous, and in removing an imaginary offence, the regulation introduces a real one.

A MAN OF ABOUT FORTY YEARS, PETERMANN RANGES.

8

THE BLACK MAN Continued

THE first interest of the Luritja is the getting of game, and his activities as a hunter have undoubtedly built into his make-up, both physical and mental, much that is most admirable, and most distinctive.

Ritual, ceremonies, magic, and the interchange of traditional lore may plays big part in the brief life of his corroborees and gatherings, but when the semi-solitary wandering which makes up most of his life is resumed, he takes up again the absorbing problem of food-getting, and becomes of necessity an intensely keen student of all that makes up the animal life of his environment. His attainments in these pursuits are extraordinary; a constant source of wonderment and admiration to all who can in any measure appreciate the difficulty of the problems he is constantly solving with certainty and ease.

His skill as a hunter is largely based on his powers of observation. These again depend on his ability to receive and retain, very swiftly, visual impressions of extraordinary minuteness of detail-a faculty which few adult whites retain, but which many children possess in greater or lesser degree.

The story of the blacks' tracking ability is one which needs no retelling here. But it may be stressed that much more is involved than mere acuteness of vision in achieving these feats, for the rapid interpretation of what is observed is even more remarkable. Many of the smaller marsupials, and, still more, many of the rodents, are so similar in point of foot structure that even when the imprint is clear and undistorted there is very often nothing which the eye of a white man can seize upon to distinguish them either in outline or disposition. Yet the blacks will unhesitatingly name the animal from its tracks; and it is very seldom that their preliminary identification based on tracks is not confirmed when the animal is ultimately hauled triumphantly from its burrow. be found that our wool-clips, and beef and timber trades have been dearly bought.

To make use of the natives as collectors; to participate actively in the business of hunting; and to have as lively an interest in the results of their work as they have themselves, is to know them under circumstances very favourable for observation. There is then no trace of the embarrassment, or awkwardness, or boredom, inevitably present in some degree when a native feels himself the object of deliberate study, and he is able to give full scope to his powers under entirely natural conditions. One may thus come to know something of the man himself in what is his chosen field, and to understand the extraordinary intimacy of his knowledge of that which he hunts. Tracking is by no means the chief of his accomplishments. In obtaining his quarry he has at his command every relevant detail of its life-history and habits, and to what he has personally seen and remembered, is added that great store of knowledge which is the communal gain of long generations of observation and deduction.

They are, indeed, specialists in animal bionomics, and experts in the taking of little lives to perpetuate their own. They follow the oldest and most fundamental of crafts; and in its reactions on their mentality and character one may see clearly mirrored the far-off beginnings of our own culture, sprung from that early time when man's chief duty and pleasure alike was a knowledge of beasts.

The digging out of small mammals is largely done by the women, and apart from the keenness which they display in locating a tenanted burrow, they are wonderfully expert in the actual work of digging and in anticipating the twists and turns of the galleries so as to avoid unnecessary work. Their only tools are a yam-stick and a *wirra*. The yam-stick is a mulga stake about four feet long, sharpened to a chisel point by carefully charring one side of one end in a slow fire and then rubbing away the charcoal on a flat whetstone until a chisel edge is formed. The *wirra* is a shallow wooden dish which functions as a sand scoop. It is extraordinary that with such simple tools they are able to make such headway.

In the business of digging out mammals the advent of the rabbit, which now swarms all over the eastern Luritja Country, has wrought great simplification, since it is far more easily procured than most of the marsupials, and is far more gregarious. As a factor in the general economy of the blacks, the importance of the rabbit as an accessory food-supply can hardly be overestimated. Its numbers fluctuate in a remarkable way in the Centre: periods when it plagues the country in swarms are followed by holocausts which render the country foul with carcasses. But it is seldom so reduced that a gin cannot find a dozen or more in a day's work. It is curious to note the reaction of the blacks to the little grey stranger, as recorded by those who have witnessed the whole history of its invasion of their country. When it first arrived in the cattle country west of Oodnadatta, about thirty-five years ago, the station blacks were amazed, and described the new-comer as a tchungooa rat-kangaroo-with ears like a donkey and tail of a "nanny-goat," and their myall brethren farther west were no doubt still more impressed. For some years they regarded the rabbit with suspicion. But once they plucked up courage to test his gastronomic possibilities and found him *kooka pauya*, he created a dietary furore, and the marsupials enjoyed unwonted peace for a while. Now, however, there has come a great revulsion. Although they still eat more of rabbits probably than of any other mammals, they do so in many cases with a comical approach to the disdain which is the typical attitude of most white Australians to *Oryctolagus*; and if there is any choice of meat offering, the native animals are always eaten in preference to the foreigner.

In a mixed camp it is *infra dig.* for a man to use a yam¬stick. Ordinarily the men's contribution to the maintenance of the group is the hunting of kangaroo, euro, rock-wallaby, and emu with the spear, and on an average, if game is plentiful, one full day in three will be devoted to hunting. The sole weapons for the purpose are the light *orichanna* or kudgee, a single-barbed throwing-spear, and the *meru* or spear-thrower. Both are well made; but as with all the rest of their simple gear, they are strictly utilitarian. They spend no time in ornamentation or unnecessary refinement, and both weapons are easily and expeditiously replaced in most localities. Arms and the man are complementary ideas with the Luritjas, and a man of full initiation seldom moves about without a "handful of hooks " - in doggers' parlance. He is not dressed without them; if he moves but twenty paces from his fireside, his spears go with him.

It is in the taking of kangaroos that the full perfection of the blacks' hunting technique is brought out best, both in their applications of animal lore and in the use of their weapons. The procedure varies a good deal with the number taking part. If a man is hunting solo, by far the most artistic if less exciting method, his aim is to get within easy throw without arousing suspicion; but if parties are out, the game, having been approached by a preliminary stalk, is driven by one section of the party towards the others, who are in ambush, and the spearing is then done "on the run." The second method is more successful with the kunala of the hills than with the merloos of the flats, and the former is sometimes killed in large numbers by being driven into an ambush. When disturbed by the beaters in a low chain of hills, the kunala will not take to the flats where there is refuge in the scrub, but keeps to the broken country as long as he can. Localities are cleverly chosen, however, in which his devotion to this habit will bring him to the terminal spur of a chain where the outcrops die away into the sand, or sometimes into a narrow pass between two chains. In either case, the euros rush almost into the arms of a concealed spearing party, who make few mistakes when they arrive.

Emus are got in somewhat similar fashion, but without the labour of driving, by planting lines of spear-men under the shelter of piles or fences of brush near suitably situated waterholes. When the big birds have overcome their first suspicions, they go down to the water to drink, and at a given signal the men rush out upon them. Piltardi, in the Petermann Hills, is a famous place for employing this device. The water is here at the foot of a perpendicular cliff and flanked by buttresses of the hills, so that a comparatively few men can hem the birds in against the walls.

A HUNTING RETURNING TO PILTARDI
Situated in prime emu country, this is a favourite camp-site of the blacks in the
Petermann Range. In the cleft near the top of the white quartz cliff are more
waterholes.

Many a long and patient wait has been crowned by a joyful butchery, there.

The blacks' quickness with their eight-foot spears is very remarkable, when it is remembered that it is never thrown "free hand," as it were, but has to be brought across the body by the left hand, and its hollowed base made to engage with the little spur on the thrower, before the cast is made. To facilitate the change-over, the spears in the left hand are always carried butt first, so that a single sweep of the arm, uncomplicated by wrist movements, will bring them into the throwing position, and the older men, who are sticklers for etiquette, when approaching you will always show their friendly intentions by reversing the shaft, and carrying the point forward.

Up to about sixty yards their accuracy is such that they will do as well as, or better than, an average good shot with either gun or rifle, on moving kangaroos or emus. But they are keenly appreciative of the advantages of a rifle. One of the shortest cuts to a place in the Luritja heart is to sit down and deliberately pull off a long shot in open country where a closer approach is impossible. Since doggers took Mannlichers and telescopic sights into the country, belief in the powers of the rifle are almost unbounded. On more than one occasion when out for meat, the blacks who were with me have begun pointing excitedly at 'roos serenely camped a mile or more away, and have sat down gleefully to watch the results of the shooting, and great is the disappointment when one endeavours to explain that there are limits to what even high velocities will do.

In some parts of the country are the remnants of game traps or corrals in the form of brush fences, in which drives on a very large scale were evidently conducted in the open country. But the practice seems to have fallen into disuse and I can hear of no recent example of such a corral having been used.

Their game killed, it is either cooked on the spot or carried into camp. Their method of carrying a kangaroo is curious, and may be of interest to those who have staggered under that most unwieldy of burdens. The animal is first gutted and its legs dislocated at the first joint.

The head is then forced down between the legs to the base of the tail, so that the trunk is flexed almost in a circle; hands, feet, and tail are then securely tied by a length of gut. A circular bundle thus results, which is hoisted on to the head and carried long distances without adjustment.

The word "cooking," as applied to the preparation of the meat, is a courtesy one only, and is used in the absence of any other to describe the process. A large fire is made on a clean sand patch, and is kept going for about an hour. The embers are then raked back, and a hollow is scooped in the hearth. Into this the viscerated carcass is lowered having first been deprived of most of its fur by scorching in the flames. It is then covered over with the hot ashes and left for about half an hour, when it is pulled out, jointed, and distributed by one of the older men. Usually the time of heating is so short that only the outer layers are cooked; the bulk of the meat is quite raw, often scarcely hot, and one marvels that the fire process is not dispensed with altogether. With small mammals the cooking is fairly effective.

Although meat bulks very large in the diet of the blacks, it is a mistake to suppose, as is often done, that vegetable foods are unimportant. The total number of edible plant products in the Centre is very considerable, and at their proper season each in turn contributes to the menu. Grass-seeds of several species are gathered, either direct or from ants' nests, and are rubbed on sandstone slabs to a rough flour, from which the gins cook damper cakes. In spite of their violent aperient action, the blacks are very fond of them. The yams are free from this defect and from a white man's point of view are much more palatable and have the great advantage of being easily gathered in quantity. Somewhat allied to the yams in flavour is the alunqua; a green cucumber-like fruit borne by a plant which climbs upon the mallee in the sand-hills.

Of the sweet fruits, the quondong and plum are first favourites. The former is very plentiful; in parts of the country forming uniform thickets covering many acres. It is of interest because it affords, I believe, one of the few cases in which an attempt is made by the blacks to preserve a perishable food-stuff for future use. The fruits are stoned, pounded, partially dried, and then pressed into cakes which are carried about for a considerable time after the harvest is over. The plum is a dark blue fruit about the size of an olive, which grows on an allied plant *(Santalum lanceolatum)*. It is greatly relished, but usually, to a European palate, has too saline a flavour to be agreeable. Like the native fig, which the blacks also gather in large quantity, it is much more palatable when dried.

Most imposing of all the native fruits, however, is the so-called orange, a *Capparis* species. Like the fig, it is seldom found far from the ranges. In the fruiting season (February and March) it betrays its presence long before it comes into view by its delicious smell. The fruit is about the size and shape of a lemon, has a leathery green skin, and is filled with yellow pulp and dark brown seeds. It has a rich, bitter-sweet flavour faintly tinged with turpentine, altogether a weird combination, but one which is an unalloyed delight to the blacks. In the sand country small fruiting shrubs spring up in profusion after a hot weather rain, and from some of them the blacks reap a rich, if very transient harvest. Best of them all is the fruit of a *Solanum* called the dol dol, kumberadda or ilboranji; about the size and having somewhat the appearance of a cape gooseberry, it is quite the best-flavoured berry to be got there.

Of special interest amongst plant products is the narcotic known variously as mingil* or okiri which is a true tobacco, derived from two or more *Nicotiana* species, which grow luxuriantly at the foot of the ranges. The leaf is dried, powdered, mixed with the ash of mulga twigs and the whole chewed into a dark green plug which, when not in use, may often be discerned tucked away behind its owner's ear. It is noteworthy that the use of a mild alkali, like lime or wood ash, in conjunction with a narcotic containing the salts of alkaloids, has been independently adopted by several widely sundered peoples.

* The word "pituri," which is used by the settlers to designate this product, has no currency amongst the blacks here. It has been derived from western Queensland, where, it is rightly applied to another plant, *Duboisia Hopwoodi*.

A sweet tooth is a leading characteristic of both sexes at all ages, and the gins go to infinite trouble to get honey and other local sweets, like the sugary exudation of the mulga twigs and the honey-ant. The latter is relished exceedingly. It is a deep burrowing ant which feeds on the mulga bloom. After rain, its abdomen becomes distended to a bladder about the size of a grape, and is filled with a thin syrup, the sweetness of which is relieved by a slight acidity and a flavour of malt. The gins will frequently do half a day's heavy digging, sometimes following the galleries four feet deep in the loam, in order to get perhaps fifty or a hundred ants.

It is a solemn moment for the gins, when at last they lay down their yam-sticks, and prepare to give themselves up to the silent enjoyment of the ravishing delicacy. One by one the feebly struggling ants are tenderly seized by the forepart, the abdomen placed between the lips, and its contents squeezed into the mouth.

It is a solemn moment for the ants, also.

MINGIL
The native tobacco, Nicotiana suaveoleus, flowering near a waterhole in the George Gill Range.

75

9

THE BLACK MAN Continued

IN taking a general survey of the blackfellow and of the life he leads, one cannot do other than devote much attention to matters of food and food-getting, since these play so important a part in his affairs, and to dwell somewhat on the curious simplicity of his material culture and his freedom from what might be called the apparatus complex, which in increasing degree marks the higher cultures of ascending civilization.

Yet it is the greatest mistake to suppose, as is so often done popularly, that these things imply a corresponding inferiority in all those matters of heart and feeling which form the basis of the moral character of men, and to hold that the aborigine, apart from specific identity, is scarcely entitled to share a common humanity with us. In recent years there has been a quickening of interest in the black man and his future. The bad old days of public and official indifference, or worse, have gone, and a growing body of the community has come to be more or less directly interested in his welfare. He no longer lacks sympathy and concern. But it must be admitted that very often it is the same sort of sympathy which might be lavished on the disappearing marsupials; and the same sort of concern which might be felt for the loss of any other valuable scientific material. Unexpressed it may be, but implicit in much that has been written is the belief that humanly speaking, he is a poor piece of work.

Justification for such views may perhaps be found in the miserable wreckage of the race which is strewn about the margins of settlement; for nothing is more striking than the swift demoralization and degeneration which follow the renunciation of his own way of life for one of dependence on whites. But the impressions derived from the unspoiled myall in his original setting are very different.

Among the Luritjas, a general kindliness of disposition is a marked trait. In their relations to one another, asperities are sometimes introduced by disputes over trespass, and in the allotting of women and by bad magic and so on; but there is little evidence of those implacable hatreds and endless blood-feuds which have convulsed other primitive peoples; or of those deliberate cruelties and lusting delight in another's pain, which, in the American peoples for example, serve to remind one that man is part fiend as well as beast.

There are barbarities enough, it is true, in their initiatory ceremonies, and features in their disposal of the aged, and of surplus children, which are terrible. But the latter are in the nature of stark necessities imposed by the whole conditions of life and are not due to any lack of feeling or sympathy for the victim. Old men and women who have been left alone to die, because they can no longer keep up in the constant treks from water to water, are mourned as sincerely as those who die in their prime; and behind the frequent slaying of the new-born, is the idea of a gain in strength to the next child.

Their attitude towards children is one of fond indulgence; and the same feeling brims over in their extravagant love of dogs and other pets. In spite of this regard, however, their dogs lead a most miserable life, since they are required to hunt all day for their masters, and then most of the night for themselves. Nowadays, too, they are liable at' short notice to be deprived of the doubtful boon of life itself and converted into a scalp, which can always be traded to a wandering dogger for an issue of flour.

The dog is a utility as well as a pet, but it is curious that the feral cat, now plentiful all over the Centre, is also an object of considerable affection. Although he finds his way to the cooking hearth pretty often, he is yet on a very different footing from the marsupials and rabbits. It is significant that the cat affords the single example of a non-indigenous mammal which has had a Luritja name applied to it; a circumstance which may indicate that it has had a much longer tenure of the country than is usually supposed; and that it made its way into the Centre long before the advent of white men there, either from the early eastern settlements or possibly from the north-west coast.

Individual temperaments vary, of course, amongst the blacks; but in general the Luritjas, though ordinarily restrained and dignified in manner, are notably good humoured. They are free from that buffoonery which cartoonists have fixed on their brethren of the east coast, but at the same time they are easily amused, and on occasion will laugh heartily in a shrill falsetto. Their sense of humour is of that simple kind which is roused by the spectacle of trifling mishaps, like a kangaroo falling over itself in its haste to escape, or a camel throwing its load, or one of their own number being nipped by a dog, and so on. Closely akin is their love of mimicry. The most minute details of mannerisms both of beast and man are remembered and reproduced in pantomime. The children are particularly acute in such matters; they will give faithful imitations of the style of walk and bearing of a man, with only the most superficial acquaintance to guide them.

Strongly at variance with the idea of their stolidity and dullness, and so characteristic of them that it survives even the corroding influence of civilization, is their love of song. I have heard the carefully-staged performances which form a background of sound to some of their corroborees, and they are boring to a degree; but quite different and unexpectedly thrilling in the sudden revelation of emotional capacities, masked in ordinary intercourse, are the spontaneous, high-spirited campfire gatherings, which follow inevitably when, in the course of their immense wanderings, parties meet unexpectedly or converge on a common water.

On three occasions I have been camped near by when such reunions have taken place, and the proceedings were substantially the same in each. They are purely recreational affairs, in no way ritualistic; musical evenings, in fact, in which men, women, and children all join. Between the singing periods they laugh and chat, but a certain decorum is preserved, and no horse-play amongst the youngsters is permitted. Two of the older men occupy the centre of the group, which is arranged around a pattern of little fires, and they always lead the chant and keep the time and stress by beating on the ground with short sticks. The chant itself is very short, occupying only a minute or so, but it is repeated with varying intensities and pitch hour after hour. It begins on a high, loud note, and then proceeds downwards to a lower, almost whispered one, with a queer wavering rhythm which is followed with unfaltering precision by every voice. The whole is sung in clanging nasal tones, very different from their soft clear speaking one.

Hedged in by solitudes, and with its setting of blue-black night sky and fire-lit mulga, the swaying, sound-drunk group completes a scene which serves to crystallize in memory much that is most characteristic in the people and their country.

With the first tattoo that breaks the silence, one's camel-boys begin to fidget by their lonely fire. It is not long before they slip away and join their brethren, and thereafter one listens alone to almost endless repetitions of the song. But into each fresh rendering such a zest of feeling is infused, that it compels one's attention long after the physical ear has tired and would be rid of the thing.

But the songs themselves are arresting. In spite of their almost skeletal simplicity, there is something in them akin to our own music; and the springs of emotion which give them origin are not strange and remote as they often seem to be, to an untrained ear, in much Oriental music. Further, each tiny song is a single rich theme, complete in itself, carried swiftly to a logical conclusion, unweakened by meanderings or side issues. It has all the artistic force of a thing free from flaw.

Correlated perhaps with their lack of a property sense, but none the less admirable for that, is the blacks' generosity and impartiality in matters of food distribution. All food obtained becomes the common property of the group, and is brought in and distributed by the older men to all who require it, regardless of any special claims which might be put forward (but never are) by the man who obtained it. Time and time again this generosity has been extended to white men *in extremis.* In the matter of water, the blacks' attitude has been almost quixotically generous, and in a country where water is a vital thing, he has shared freely with the invader and his ravenous stock. True, he may not disclose all his sources of supply.

THE METHOD OF CARRYING HEAVY GAME INTO CAMP AFTER
SPEARING, BASEDOW RANGE

But after sixty years of experience have taught him the serious depletion which a string of camels may cause to the smaller rock-holes and soaks, he cannot be blamed for that.

An episode is related which bears interestingly on this and on the blacks' frequent altruism in the relations of the two people. Some years ago, on a prospecting trip south-west of the Tomkinson, two doggers got into serious difficulties through water shortage. On the point of turning back they fell in with a party of blacks who not only showed them where their local supply was, but piloted them onwards three days into the sand-hill country to the last soak they knew. Beyond this, they explained, they could not go, and they strongly urged the prospectors not to venture into country where their own people had often gone and had not returned. Both they and their camels, they explained, with dramatic detail, would surely die and no one see them more. But when the two, having filled their canteens, prepared to push on alone, the four older men drew apart a little, and, sitting down, wept quietly before beginning their own return journey.

It is, in fact, in their dealings with white men that the blacks' attributes of fairness and truth are thrown most strongly into relief. Surely in no other country in the world, have the aboriginal people assisted so materially in facilitating the process of European occupation-and so frequently to their own undoing! From the very first days of exploration in the Centre, their services as guides, finders of water, and trackers of stock have been freely used. And all too often they have been requited with abuse and sneers.

On the admittedly difficult question of the present relations of white man to black in the areas of pastoral settlement, much may be said on both sides. As I have pointed out, the blackfellow of the inside country tends to be a very different person from the myall. It is too much to expect that men, battling for a livelihood, should take a patient view of the numerous exasperations to which they are occasionally subject by the presence of blacks on country which the law permits them to hold. But it is amazing that so many otherwise reasonable and fair-minded men should shut their minds to the ultimate cause of all friction; and while calmly assuming all rights in the country, refuse to admit any responsibility or obligation to the people who have been dispossessed.

There are exceptions, of course, to every rule. A small minority of settlers are ready to champion the native and resist invasion of his rights, even at the cost of local odium and unpopularity; and it is generally true that the private attitude of individual settlers is much less harsh than that which they see fit to adopt in the company of their fellows. But a sort of perverted loyalty to a fixed and adverse public opinion amongst them, dries up the springs of sympathy and understanding. Men who may be models of right dealing and good fellowship with their white brethren, are ashamed to speak well of the black man, and maintain, in public, an aloofness from him and an ignorance or contempt of his language and customs, curiously at variance with the real condition of intimacy and semi-independence which frequently exists between them.

A logical outcome of this is the eagerness with which occasional real misdemeanours of the natives are seized and advanced as evidence of the depravity of the whole race. Such misdemeanours do, of course, occur; on two occasions I myself have had to contend with what appeared to be the deliberate treachery of myalls who had been well and fairly treated. No doubt even undisturbed blackfellow communities have their "tough guys" as well as our own; though that is poor ground for condemning them as a people. But if the whole story of these apparently unprovoked aggressions were known, it would be found in many cases that the gun-waving tactics of some predecessor who had attempted to conceal fear by effrontery, was the real cause of the trouble, and that endeavours on the part of a new-comer to establish relations on a better footing had been construed as weakness and a favourable opportunity for reprisals.

All who have followed the past history of the blacks in the Centre and have had opportunities of forming independent judgments, must be seized with shame at the whole ungenerous business. But let us not make the mistake in the cities of smugly repudiating responsibility and laying the whole charge of injustice upon that small section of our population in contact with the native. The settler is too heavily engaged in grappling with his own problems to view those of the aborigine in their proper perspective, and much of the wrong which has been done has accrued automatically, as it were, through the absence of effective legislation at critical junctures in the black man's story.

The problem of adjusting relations with the aborigine is really a dual one, for the myall and the detribalized black man are now worlds apart. To the handful of myalls that remain, our plain duty is to reduce all interference with their ways of life, to a minimum - regardless of how benevolent in design such projected interference may appear. And to their brethren of the settlements, alms and a patient charity, while they are with us.

But the debt we owe them is for the whole white community to discharge. That it may be done soon, and done with an open hand, must be the earnest wish of all who set justice above expediency.

DISCUSSING THE WESTERN WATERS WITH A GROUP OF BLACKS
IN THE PETERMANN RANGE
The camel-boy in the centre is interpreting.

10

CALOPRYMNUS

PECULIAR features of the Australian mammal fauna are its comparative instability as a faunal unit and the wide fluctuations to which it is constantly subject in numbers and constitution. There is a waxing and waning with varying seasons; species are common in some years, rare in others; and when they are not met with over a long series of years they become either actually, or in the book sense, "extinct." From this last condition, however, there have been some mysterious recoveries and, more than once, "extinct" species have suddenly reappeared, to the natural exasperation of authors who have taken a gloomy view. Many cases might be quoted, but the latest and most startling example is the resurrection of the Plain Rat-kangaroo, *Caloprymnus campestris*.

This remarkable animal was made known to science in 1843 by John Gould, who based his descriptions upon three specimens sent home from an unknown locality in South Australia to the British Museum by the Governor of the day, Captain George Grey. Since then, in spite of the fact that it is an animal of many peculiar characters, differing markedly from its nearest allies, and therefore a valuable desideratum in any scientific collection, no further specimens have been taken.

The first hint that the animal might still be extant was obtained in November 1930, when Mr L. Reese, who was collaborating with the writer in a survey of the mammals of the Diamantina, gave an account of an animal called by the blacks oolacunta, which was suggestive of *Oaloprymnus*. In September 1931, evidence of a more definite character was forthcoming, and, since it was a matter of the utmost importance to obtain promptly and at first hand details of its habits and distribution and photographs of the living animal, Mr Reese, at my request, made a reconnaissance of the whole district, and selected a site for future work, round which the animal seemed to be concentrating.

In December the writer proceeded up the Birdsville track to Pandi Pandi, eighteen miles from the Queensland border, and thence east to Appamunna, Reese's picturesque homestead, seven hundred miles north of Adelaide. During the next three days preparations were made in assembling plant, overhauling gear, and repacking breakables. Only those who have entrusted their cherished and indispensable belongings to the tender mercies of pig-rooting packhorses and the vicious pressure of a surcingle, can appreciate the anxiety of those last moments. Casting one's bread upon the waters is an act of calculating foresight compared with entrusting jars of formalin to a packhorse. But there was no help for it; so after some minor mishaps and readjustments, we got away on the ride into the oolacunta country.

The party consisted of Reese, myself, and four blacks - two of them Wonkonguroo horse-boys, one Wonkonguroo hunter, and one Yalliyanda hunter. "Lou" Reese is a name to conjure with in these parts. For thirty-five years he has been one of the best-known figures on the Diamantina, both on the South Australia and Queensland sides, and from Marree to Bedourie his name stands for all that is expert in stock-raising and all that is most finished in bushmanship. Less well known locally, however, are his valuable and generous services to natural science over a long series of years. In anthropology, botany, entomology, birds and mammals, he has made constant contributions in data and material, and his name figures in most of the scientific work which has been published on the natural history of the region. He was the one man who could give effective help in organizing such a quest, and he gave it with an open hand.

Great care had been taken in the selection of the blacks, as there were good reasons for keeping the party small; and we wanted no "duds." The horse-boys knew "nantos" from A to Z, and were good trackers, keen on the job. Where early starts make all the difference between relative comfort and discomfort, good temper and irritation, success and "no results," these qualities are priceless. The Yalliyanda boy, Butcher, we took chiefly because he was the only native in the district who had first-hand knowledge of oolacuntas. But the Wonkonguroo hunter, Jimmy, was our mainstay. The original blacks of this part of the Diamantina district were Yalliyandas, but they have now been supplanted almost entirely by the Wonkonguroos, themselves an offshoot of the Aruntas, occupying until recently what is known as the mickerie country, a desolation to the north-west of the Yalliyandas. Jimmy was one of the last to forsake the mickeries for the easier conditions of the cattle country, and the long struggle to support existence on the native life of a real desert, had developed in him amazing skill as a hunter of small mammals. All mammals up here smaller than a kangaroo are "rats" in local phrase, and hence Jimmy was everywhere the "rat boss. "

The country traversed on our way out to our working camp is a typical section of the Diamantina area; one of the weirdest districts in Australia. A vast succession of sand-ridges, north and south in direction and fiery red in colour, except near the channels and great flood plains, where the whole land surface is bleached to a pale yellow ochre. Between the sand-hills are either clay-pans or gibber plains, and away from the channels the vegetation is so sparse and lowly that it does nothing to hide the great nakedness of the land. Towards noon the heat and luminosity become terrific, and at our first lunch camp, looking out from the shade of a coolabah into the still, silent glare, I thought that no better picture of arid sterility could be painted. Yet it is by no means so.

Some months before, general rains had broken a drought of several years' duration, and in spite of appearances to the contrary, the herbage (judged by the standards of the country) was plentiful. The vegetation, moreover, is remarkably nutritious, and its restoration had been followed by a quick resurgence of animal life, leading ultimately to one of those plagues of rodents so characteristic of the Lake Eyre basin. During the day there is little evidence of such; but at night with the going of the sun, the country springs to life and half a dozen species of mammals swarm; several of them, like the rats called miaroo and pallyoora, (*Rattus villosissimus* and *Pseudomys minnie,* respectively) invading the camp without fear and raiding the pack-bags.

We "pulled off" finally on a little stony plain with scattered salt-

saltbush, and made our depot camp under some corkwoods. We were five miles from water, but the boys seemed so assured that the country was "right," that we decided to endure the discomforts of a waterless camp for the benefit of being near the coveted *Caloprymnus*. But I had grave misgivings. All the five bettongs that are the nearest allies of the oolacunta, I have seen in the country of their choice, and anything less promising than this stony, shelterless plain in the blaze of midsummer, would be difficult to imagine. But the blacks were right.

The plan of campaign had been anxiously debated all the way in from Appamunna, The great open sweep of the country is so immense, that all methods of procedure partook somewhat of hunting for a needle in a haystack. Snaring and trapping were out of the question, shooting was too damaging to skeletons, and the most practicable method (while the horses lasted) seemed to be for the whole party to beat up the country mounted, and gallop anything which was put up.

At this juncture Butcher created a sensation by announcing that he could catch oolacuntas by hand. When questioned, he explained that many years ago when "big mob jump up alonga Barcoo," the blacks used to locate the grass nests and then, determining the direction in which the opening lay, would, if the wind were right, sneak up behind and, silently slipping a coolamon or their hands over the top, bag the occupant! Some jealousy existed between Butcher and Jimmy, and Reese and I were inclined to attribute this account to a desire to shine. Moreover, there was a certain Alice-in-Wonderlandish touch about this method of capture by the "laying on of hands." So much so, that Reese, on reflection, was constrained to administer a grave rebuke to Butcher, suggesting indeed, that he was a sanguinary liar. But in this we wronged him.

Seldom do the things one keenly desires come easily.

But on our very first cast we got a prize. The six of us rode east in the early morning, and on a sand-hill picked up fresh oolacunta tracks crossing to a flat on the far side. We followed them out till we lost them in the gibbers; then we opened out to a half-mile front and rode slowly south, each man scanning every lump and tussock for a possible nest. We had ridden less than half an hour when there came a shrill excited "Yuchai"

STURT'S STONY DESERT

An early morning view from the western edge, showing the glare on the gibbers; pack-horses on the horizon. It is on the fringes of this type of country that *Caloprymnus* lives.

THE OOLACUNTA
As he appears at speed.

from the horse-boy farthest out, and the chase was on. The pre-arranged plan was for each of us to take up the galloping in turn, the rat being headed whenever possible and turned in towards the rest of the party who remained in a group. When the first horse showed signs of losing heart, the next man took the first opportunity of replacing him, and so on.

Following the yell, Tommy came heading back down the line towards the sand-hill, but it was only after much straining of eyes that the oolacunta could be distinguished - a mere speck, thirty or forty yards ahead. At that distance it seemed scarcely to touch the ground; it almost floated ahead in an eerie, effortless way that made the thundering horse behind seem, by comparison, like a coal hulk wallowing in a heavy sea.

They were great moments as it came nearer; moments filled with curiosity and excitement, but with a steady undercurrent of relief and satisfaction. It was here! *Caloprymnus* bears a strong external resemblance to five or six other related species and from a distance there was little to distinguish that which was approaching from either of two other marsupials known to occur in adjoining tracts. But as it came down the flat towards me, a little pale ghost from the 1840s, all doubt fled. The thing was holding itself very differently from the bettongs. As I watched it through the shimmering heat haze, some sense of the incongruous brought back a vivid memory of a very different scene, two years before, when I had sought the nearest living relative of *Oaloprymnus*, above the snow-line on a Tasmanian range

Imagine a little animal about the bulk of a rabbit, but built like a kangaroo, with long spindly hind legs, tiny fore-legs folded tight on its chest, and a tail half as long again as the body but not much thicker than a lead pencil, and you have it in the rough. But its head, short and blunt and wide, is very different from that of any kangaroo or wallaby, and its coat is uniformly coloured a clear pale yellowish ochre - exactly like the great clay-pans and flood plains.

As it came up to us I galloped alongside to keep it under observation as long as possible. Its speed, for such an atom, was wonderful, and its endurance amazing. We had considerable difficulty in heading it with fresh horses. When we finally got it, it had taken the starch out of three mounts and run us twelve miles; all under such adverse conditions of heat and rough going, as to make it almost incredible that so small a frame should be capable of such an immense output of energy. All examples obtained subsequently by this method behaved similarly; they persisted to the very limit of their strength, and quite literally, they paused only to die.

Back at the camp all was jubilation, The afternoon and most of next day were spent in examining, sketching, photographing, measuring, dissecting, and preserving - for luck is not to be trusted. And I wanted to make the very most of the first specimen lest it be also the last. We rode out each day, sometimes to success, sometimes not. In the afternoons we worked on the rats which the "rat boss" had dug, while the heat under the corkwoods grew ever worse and worse. Even the old hands, reared under the grim old tradition of "salt beef, damper, and constipation," who love to hark back to the summers when it really *was* hot, admitted subsequently that it had been bad. I had thought the still days bad, but when the hot winds came I thought again. When the flies and ants and heat and sand could be endured no longer, we left the skinning and spelled. And while we gazed out over the white-hot flats and sand-hills, we sipped boiling tea, and had torturing visions of iced Quellthaler in an old-time shady garden.

On the day before we broke camp to start on the long ride to Cordilla and the Innamincka track, Butcher quashed for ever the soft impeachment which Reese had made on his veracity and covered himself with glory.

It was usual for two of the boys to take the horses to water each evening near sundown, and fill the canteens at the hole five miles away. On this afternoon they had been gone no more than half an hour when Butcher rode back into camp alone. With impassive face and in dignified silence, he handed over a bag tied at the mouth. Very cautious investigation showed it to contain a beautiful fully-adult oolacunta and a half-grown joey - both alive and undamaged. Those we had run down were too exhausted to make good life-studies for a camera, but here were

90

fitting subjects at last.

In riding over the country, we had had ample confirmation of Butcher's statement about the nest-building habit of *Oaloprymnus*. In a fiery land, where a burrowing habit is the chief factor in the survival of most species, the oolacunta clings pathetically to a flimsy shelter of grass and leaves, which it makes in a shallow depression scratched out of the loam. And now, here was a splendid proof of his second claim. The Yalliyanda boy had, while riding with the others, spotted a nest and noted the head of the occupant in the opening, watching the party. He rode on without pause for a quarter of a mile, then, leaving his horse, made a rapid stalk up the wind and grabbed both mother and babe from behind.

The laying on of hands was no myth!

* The episode described in this chapter occurred in the Lake Eyre basin, in surroundings very different from those of the Luritja Country, six hundred miles to the west. It will be understood, therefore, that some of the statements in the earlier chapters on the physical features of the south-western centre, do not apply here.

THE POTOROO *(POTOROUS TRIDACTYLUS)*
A wet country animal, but the nearest living ally of the Oolacunta.

11

THE CAMEL

MAN, in his boast of a conquest of nature, is not generally disposed to share the glory with the beasts of burden, which have been one of his chief instruments in the undertaking.

In the long upward struggle to the age of the machine, nothing is stranger, nothing more humiliating, than the realization that man himself has borne but a small part of the brunt of the strife, and the beasts a very large one. Happily, this phase of his dependence is passing, particularly in the towns where now it is easy to forget that there is a debt. But who has not heard at some time the scream of a horse in a street accident, and in hearing, has not sensed uneasily that dark abyss of animal pain, over which man has reared the pleasance of his civilization.

It is a far cry from a dingy street to the sunlit wastes of the Centre. Yet the history of its "conquest" is so largely a story of the endurance and sufferings of horses and camels, and they are so closely identified with life there to-day, that no picture of the country is complete without them. Beyond the pastoral zone the horse is now little more than a memory of the first explorers. But the camel is supreme, a necessity of life and work, and to almost every experience of the country which one may bring to mind, there clings some memory of the tall beast that bears for one the heat and burden of the day.

In a country where so many faunal introductions have been disastrous, the camel, so far, is a grateful exception. Since its first use upon extended journeys in the Centre by Gosse and Warburton in 1873 and by Giles in 1876, its history in the dry country has been one of almost unqualified success. The reasons for this success are largely anatomical and physiological, but partly temperamental as well, and they are best brought out perhaps by comparisons with the horse. The comparison is an interesting one, for though the characteristics of both species were stamped upon them by an arid steppe environment, the horse in his long sojourn in Western Europe under easier conditions, seems to have lost most of his xerophile traits, and over large portions of the Centre he is a signal failure. But the horse and his use are so closely woven with the history of the human race, that sentiment and aesthetic appeal lead to a glossing over of his many defects, and in a land strongly committed to horse craft, the camel, as an alien, has won his triumph in the face of scornful prejudice. Not until one has had to depend on him under circumstances where he was the deciding factor between safety and disaster, does one appreciate fully his sterling qualities and realize how superficial and unfair are those criticisms which bulk so large in our Natural Histories.

The two chief advantages of the horse are speed and mobility. Under suitable conditions he will cover in a day fifty to one hundred per cent more ground than a camel; and he will take all types of country in his stride - rocks, sand, and scrub. The Arabian camel, on the other hand, is definitely specialized in foot structure to soft, even surfaces and though by dint of much 'wangling" he can be got over some extraordinarily rough places, yet he is a source of some anxiety in the hills owing to his uncertain foothold and the damage so easily done to his soft feet and pointed nails. The Bactrian camel,* with his shorter limbs and harder feet, might make a better showing in the ranges, though at the cost of still shorter daily stages. The advantage of speed, however

* C. bactriamus was introduced in the early 1890s, and Phillipson writing in 1895 stated that there were then five in Australia. A male and female of this species were worked for some years by the late Price Maurice at Mount Eba in South Australia, but apparently never become thoroughly acclimatized and subsequently died in the Zoological Gardens at Adelaide. In 1902 some of the hybrid progeny of this bull, out of Arabian cows, were travelled by R. T. Maurice from Ooldea to the Cambridge Gulf. No details, however, of their performance as compared with the rest of the team, seem to have been published.

is one which tends to diminish on long trips, since a horse-plant must be spelled more frequently than camels and if mileages are checked up week by week there is no great advantage in favour of horses. But even making full allowance for these, they are offset by so many disabilities, that horse traverses, in all but the most favoured districts of the Centre, are fraught with anxiety in summer; an anxiety which hung like a pall over every experience of the early explorers.

Of the many reasons for the success of the camel, undoubtedly the most fundamental (as it is the best known) is his ability to endure drought. But under present day conditions this is somewhat less important than formerly, and it is not generally understood that his drought-resisting properties are only brought out. to the full by careful education.

If taken on a long dry stage in hot weather, after a period of regular watering, he will soon show signs of distress, and if opportunity offers, will drink enormously. A gelded male which I travelled with a light pack from Piltardi in the Petermann to Oparinna in three and a half days in very hot weather, on arrival at the springs, drank thirty-three gallons measured out in three-gallon tins, before he paused, and then after a quarter of an hour, a further ten gallons. A light riding cow on the same occasion took twenty-five gallons as a first instalment, followed by another five gallons after a short interval. In hot weather, four days travelling without water would probably bring unseasoned pack-camels to dire straits, though even so, his performance is very superior to that of the horse. But if in hard working trim, he will go six or eight days without a drink and there are instances of camels travelling constantly and with full loads surviving seventeen days' drought on the dryest of feed. These feats are exceptional, but a week's "dry" is fairly common.

On the other hand a horse, three days without water, is very likely to be a dead horse, and is certainly a useless horse so far as getting on with the job is concerned. Most ordinarily bred horses are not "bitter 'enders" and they show signs of throwing up the sponge long before their chances of pulling through are gone and adversity, which mirrors a camel to best advantage, tends to show up all that is worst in horses. There are few experiences more harrowing than an attempt to drive packhorses once they have made up their minds they are beaten; and few memories one would more gladly forget than that of a "quitter" unsaddled and shot; or, less mercifully perhaps, turned adrift to take his chance of making his way back to the last water.

Now that the era of exploration is past and the location of the main waters is known, feed, and feeding habits, become of even greater importance than water, and probably the most valuable trait of the camel is the extraordinary catholicity of his taste in food plants, for there is scarcely any plant, small or great, in the Centre, which he does not lay under toll with evident relish. Some of them are singularly unattractive to outward seeming, like the spiny *Bassias* and *Solanums*, and many are utterly nauseous to the human palate and shunned even by goats. A notable example is the woody, bright orange fruit of the white wood, *Atalaya* sp., which is intolerably bitter but which the camels will seek out and eagerly devour. For the most part he is a browser. His great height and flexible neck are valuable specializations for seizing and dragging down the twigs and bushy tops of small trees and large shrubs; and, quantitatively, the almost ubiquitous arborescent mulga is his most valuable supply. Of the small herbaceous plants, the deliciously succulent parakeelia calls for comment as it frequently leads to one's downfall while on the move with a "string." A clump of parakeelia has for a camel much the same attraction as fruit hanging over a garden wall has for a small boy; however resolutely one keeps them at the job, sooner or later one of the string will not be able to resist the temptation to snatch a mouthful of the luscious stuff, and crack goes a nose line. While the offender is being brought back into the line, his comrades seize the opportunity to do a little foraging for themselves, all in different directions. The inevitable calves, the quintessence of mischief, now wander up to their dams for light refreshment, and in a trice the whole string is in a tangle. Parakeelia is a beautiful plant to camp on, but when in a hurry - well, not so beautiful.

Dreaded for more serious reasons is the deadly camel poison, *Duboisia Hopwoodi.* Camels which are strangers to it eat it freely and with fatal results; but when reared in notorious poison belts, they either learn to

WATERING CAMELS BY BALING FROM AN INACCESSIBLE ROCK-HOLE
Illillinna: West of the Everard Ranges.

PALS
A camel-boy from the Musgraves, with one of his pets.

it or acquire an immunity from its effect. Still more deadly, but fortunately rarer, are the pretty blue-flowered *Isotoma patraea*, *Myoporum deserti*, and *Gastrolobium grandiflorum*.

The horse, by comparison, is highly selective in his feeding, and has a strong preference for grasses and small herbaceous plants. He can make little use, even if he would, of the much more plentiful "top feed;" so, it will often come about that camels will do well in country where horses starve. When travelling with horses, this peculiarity of their feeding bears heavily on one's own plans, since one's camps must be selected almost entirely with reference to their needs.

Less directly, the difficulties of water and feed are responsible for other minor but very exasperating troubles which detract greatly from the usefulness of horses.

When camp is made in the evening, it is the custom to hobble both horses and camels and turn them loose to feed. under the occasional surveillance of the "boys." The whole business is casual to a degree, but is necessary in order to give as complete a degree of freedom as possible for feeding, and, in the case of camels, works well enough as they are usually content to feed the night through over a small area with frequent intervals of rest. But if the camp is a dry one, horses are very apt to make an attempt to get back to the last water, and so retrace much of the ground won during the day. In such a case one sits in camp with what patience one can muster, while the horse-boys pick up the tracks in the morning and bring the truants in-perhaps too late to make a start that day.

In this horse and camel hunting, the blacks are supremely useful. True, a white man *can* do the work. But to leave camp when there is light enough to see, to spend the whole morning perhaps, breakfastless under a blistering sun until the cantankerous beasts are located and brought together, and then to find one's way back to the heap of saddles dropped on a featureless mulga plain which constitutes a "camp," is a proceeding which most white men leave very gladly to the "lesser folk." I have tried it; and I know.

There are certain obvious precautions which can be taken in avoiding these delays and annoyances; such, for instance, as watching the beasts more closely and keeping a horse near the camp in readiness for a possible hunt next morning. These precautions can be and are taken with camels, for a camel in Australia is a mere utility without a tradition. But do not suggest to a bushman of the old school doing any of these things with horses. There is a certain code of etiquette in the working of horses-it is a craft with formal technique. There are things which are done, and things which are not done, and it is better by far that one should waste a perfectly good day in horse hunting than that one should lose caste by resigning something of that careless nonchalance so necessary in a horse master. More practical considerations apply however, in mustering and droving camps, where the "night horse" is an invariable institution.

A third group of advantages accrues from the superior strength of the camel. A bull camel will carry from five to seven hundredweight day after day, week after week, without being in any way taxed, while an average packhorse in midsummer may knock up with two hundred pounds.

In travelling with horses this imposes on one certain limitations, not only as to the weight which can be carried, but how it is packed. The soft leather pack-bags afford no protection whatever to one's gear which must take its chance of being kicked to pieces, scraped off on tree-trunks or rolled on in waterholes. Moreover, since any lack of balance in the packs leads to frenzied attempts on the part of the horse to get rid of his load, the distribution of weight in the two bags becomes the deciding factor in packing and it is impossible to follow any rational scheme of arrangement. At the end of the day's ride, when one's patience is not at its strongest, one must rummage amongst a most incongruous association of objects in order to find what one wants.

Then, too, with limited carrying capacity one realizes quickly that it is not only armies that travel on their bellies. It may be humiliating, but it is very true, that one's food is likely to have a profound effect on one's outlook and mental condition. "Tucker," with a horse-plant small enough to make good time, tends to degenerate rather rapidly into flour, tea, and what you can get with a rifle, and although there are hardy spirits amongst the old timers who scoff at any additions as superfluous, yet it must be confessed that one is apt to lose interest on such a diet, and to one unused to it, the mere act of ingesting sufficient damper to maintain strength is by no means easy.

These things may seem small, but their cumulative effect is not, and thus it comes about that memory paints two very different pictures of experiences with horses. On a short trip, in cool weather, in a country of good feed and plentiful water, all goes well and no day is too long. You get away from your camps early, and after a good night men and beasts are brisk and the lust of life is strong in all. The packs forge ahead whinnying signals to the saddle-horses, and as they bustle through the mulga, there is a jolly crash of sticks and jingle of hobble-rings, tossing of heads and play of heels. It is a day to justify the old saying of the cattle-men, that a man was given legs so that he could throw them over a horse's back.

But in midsummer, in the dry sand country, and after some weeks out, what a change! There is an air of gloom and a sense of strain. Through the long hot day you ride in a cloud of fine dust and the clinking of the hobbles wears on your nerves more than would be thought possible. At sundown, off-saddle in a dry camp very likely, with damper and tea, squatting on your heels in the dust, as a preliminary to lying down in sweaty clothes, wondering if you will ever sleep again. Then in the morning, the usual circus of saddling and packing sulky horses, and on again.

With camels, weight, within wide limits, is not a press¬ing consideration, and equipment can be planned on a much more generous scale. Packing is a simple matter, since all small articles are carried in stout wooden boxes in place of flimsy pack-bags, and though balancing is necessary, it is much more easily carried out than with horse-packs, and lack of it does not usually lead to such speedily disastrous results as with horses. Adjustments of all kinds, moreover, are much easier since your camels, padding along in single file, are always within reach, as it were, and when told to "uish," have the accommodating habit of folding up their legs and coming to rest on their bellies with the loads no more than waist high. Pack-horses by contrast are very inaccessible, since they are usually driven ahead of the riding party; and their freedom is curtailed only by the horse-boys who ride at the flanks of the "mob." To get at a pack the boys must head the mob, "hold" them, and catch the horse required; not always easy things to do.

A minor disadvantage attending the use of the bigger beast, is the unwieldiness of the saddles, boxes, and canteens generally used, all of which are much heavier and more bulky than the corresponding horse gear. This is of small moment when plenty of hands are available, as they usually are, but it becomes a serious matter in an emergency if one is forced to travel alone. A quiet packhorse can be loaded single handed without much trouble. But to load a camel "solo" is seldom easy and sometimes calls for some hard thinking, as well as considerable persistence. The pack-saddles are mountainous structures consisting essentially of wooden supports and two straw-stuffed pads shaped to rest snugly on either side of the hump, which protrudes between them. They are provided with crupper and neck-strap, but no girths or surcingle, and can be rolled off sideways, with little hindrance.

Ordinarily the two balanced side loads go on simul¬taneously, being held in position by two men, one of whom then ties the rope sling which suspends the packs across the saddle. But when alone, the two parts must perforce go up singly. When the first is strapped in position it must at once be propped up with sticks, rocks, boxes, flour butts, or whatever is available, to prevent its weight pulling the saddle off, while one dashes round to the opposite side to get its fellow into position. The least movement of the camel during the change over suffices to capsize the wobbly props and then away goes the whole affair, saddle, packs, props, and ropes in a wild tangle.

When this has happened two or three times, the quietest camel gets a little upset and decides to stand up. It is then incumbent on one to speak soothing words to him, and coax him to his knees once more, so that one may begin again, and if necessary still again. It is a job which can

100

be confidently recommended as a discipline for the impatient.

The riding position of the Eastern countries, perched. right on the hump, has been abandoned in Australia for a slightly lower one between the hump and the hind catup of the saddle. Even so, one is several feet higher than on horseback; no small advantage in heavy scrubs, where one may ride a horse for days and scarcely see a horizon.

The gait of the camel has generally been held up to scorn by horsemen; and much has been said about the discomfort of camel riding. It may be so for stockily-built people, and the movements of ambling are certainly peculiar, but the long swinging walk is more restful than any pace of a horse. Well that it is so; since, although light riding-camels will amble at seven to ten miles an hour, pack-camels will not do more than three miles an hour, even when the going is good. This means travelling practically from dawn till dark to average thirty miles per day.

But that is a small price to pay for many blessings.

12

THE CAMEL Continued

WHEN all the pros and cons of practical utility have been debated (and the argument is one dear to the bushman's heart), horse advocates are wont to console themselves with reflections on the supposed aesthetic and temperamental shortcomings of the camel. He is, they will assure you, an evil beast; dirty, malodorous, stupid, ugly, and vicious.

Well, certainly he has a fine carelessness in the disposal of his waste products; and after he has fed all night on gidgee or buckbush, he exhales a fume which quite justifies the name "stinker," freely applied to him in the Centre.

But with regard to his stupidity, one is on difficult ground. For the question of intelligence, even in domesticated animals, is one which admits of great latitude of opinion even amongst neurologists, who have a firmer basis for their conclusions than the casual observation of behaviour. Man is apt to hail as intelligent those animals, like the horse and dog, which bend easily to his will; and feelings of pique have operated in attributing stupidity to those which, like the camel, remain to some extent aloof and indifferent to him.

It is surely more just to judge intelligence by the success with which species serve their own interests, rather than those of man. When camels are freed from human interference and left to fend for themselves, they manage their affairs in the bush with great success and with frequent evidence of intelligence. Horses, on the other hand, judged by the same standards, sometimes make a poor showing. There are well authenticated instances of strong horses dying of thirst on a drying clay-pan, while a permanent water, with which they were familiar, was twenty miles away. And at least one example of a pair of horses, which fed their way slowly to the top of a craggy tent hill, and there perished because they could not find their way down the scarp again.

Examples of great stupidity and great sagacity could be cited for both animals, but it is mere prejudice which assigns the first to the camel and the second to the horse as an exclusive possession.

Temperamentally, the camel is less exuberant than the horse and preserves an outward impassiveness through good times and bad, very different from the mercurial ups and downs of *Equus*. But this stolidity is an outward thing only and in reality he is quite as sensitive as the lesser beast, and his reactions to kindness and cruelty are of the same kind.

As to beauty - who shall decide - Europeans committed to the horse, may condemn the camel; but it is significant that other peoples who make use of both, see beauty in both, and when a Bedouin chief compares the charms of his best beloved to those of a cow camel, it seems hardly necessary to look to irony as the source of the comparison. Whatever one's first impressions, familiarity with his lines and understanding of his ways of locomotion, lead quickly to an opinion entirely favourable.

There remains the question of viciousness. There is a great array of anecdote bearing on this; of men bitten and struck down by passing camels with no provocation; of sleeping men sought out in their camps and crushed to death; and of the snarling, menacing demeanour of most camels when approached even with the most harmless of intentions. Some of this relates to sex-mad bulls; but a good deal of what remains is undoubtedly true. As evidence of the disposition of the camel as a species, however, it is worthless, unless considered with an understanding of the conditions under which camels are worked.

Riding-camels which are objects of pride and individual attention from their owners are in a category apart. But in the last sixty years enough has been seen in this country, of the revolting cruelties which frequently attended the use of pack-camels by incompetent teamsters, to throw a flood of light on the origin of the "viciousness" which is so much blamed. Of these abuses, overloading was perhaps the worst, and the horrors which follow the overloading of camels will not bear detailed description. When properly packed and adjusted, the pressure of the load is taken chiefly by the ribs, but if the weight is excessive or. the saddle maladjusted, the hump takes most of the punishment and the great mass of soft, fatty tissue becomes one huge bruise. In a hot climate this is at once discovered by flies, and if neglected, there follows a destruction of tissue in the living beast, on such a scale as to wring a shudder from the most hardened of men.

Then there is the torture of the nose-peg. The peg is a hardwood cylinder expanding to a disk at one end and a smaller pointed cone at the other. In inserting it for the first time, the young camel is thrown, the cartilage of the left nostril pierced with a steel probe, and the peg pushed through the wound so that the base rests upon the inner surface of the wing of the nostril, and the cone, to which the nose-line is subsequently attached, projects beyond.

In riding-camels, and with gentle handling, the device is perhaps not more cruel than some others which have the general sanction of the humane. But handling is not always gentle and with abuse, the peg may become a barbarous affliction, leading to inflamed and suppurative conditions and constant pain. On approaching a string of kneeling camels which have been mishandled, a babel of weird noises at once breaks out, before an animal is touched; roars and snarls and a guttural rattle, all very unpleasant and usually accompanied by a baring of teeth and other menacing movements. These demonstrations, probably more than anything else, have given rise to the idea of the camel's ill-temper; but the thing is no more than a nervous reaction to the dread of the pain which has so often befallen them, when rude hands have laid hold of the line.

That this is so, is virtually proved by the general absence of these demonstrations in camels bred and educated and exclusively worked by men of patience and understanding. In a string of such there are nearly always one or two "old" pets who will give one a very different greeting. As one comes alongside they begin a little ceremony of playful obeisance, lowering their heads little by little till at last the whole neck and head lie flat upon the sand. They are inviting you to scratch their ears, which done, they purr happily like huge cats and then prepare to push on with the work.

Apart from man-made troubles, however, the camel is prone to several of his own and there is a true Oriental lavishness in the poor brute's affiictions, for boils, abscesses, mange, and other conditions assume dimensions and virulence staggering to our Western ideas of stock diseases.

The more one inquires into the conditions and practices which have moulded the camel's lot in the past, and which have so often converted a baggage train under the old regime into a walking hell, the less one wonders at the peevishness of the brute and the more at his endurance and strength. But a new day is dawning for the camel, and his future in this country promises to make a welcome contrast to his tragic past. The Afghan no longer has a monopoly of camel craft. More and more Europeans in the Centre are breeding their own animals and applying rational methods to his education and use, and the results are at once apparent in changing over from a disaffected string to one which has never been abused.

A long trip with such camels is the surest way of removing prejudice and replacing it with esteem, and only thus can one glimpse something of the quaintness and pathos of the great beast, "half orphan child" perhaps, as Kipling thought, but surely no devil.

Of the many whimsical traits which unspoiled camels possess, one of the most interesting is their attachment to certain localities; and they have a curious method of signalling their satisfaction at a home-coming to such places. I remember well my first experience of this.

We were heading for a camp in the Everard forty miles away, with a string of twenty-two "humps," and steering for a far-distant conical hill rising solitary out of the usual mulga sea. It was a day of appalling heat made worse by a hot north wind. Camels are always irritable in winds. Maybe some racial memory of the sand blizzards of the old world deserts stirs uneasily at such times. They became increasingly restless as the day advanced, and by mid-afternoon the youngsters refused to face it any longer. So we decided to camp till the worst was over and go on by night.

GOATS IN THE FAR NORTH-WEST OF SOUTH AUSTRALIA

BEGINNING THE DAY
Camels and horses coming in to water on Deception Creek, James Range.

The wind dropped at sundown and the night was quiet and moonlit, with a few fleecy clouds drifting across. At midnight we got the camels in and started again.

They are different beasts. Almost at once they settle into their stride and hour after hour they slip along, without check or break of rhythm, and with no sound but the soft stirring of the sand underfoot. The silence grows uncanny. Twenty tons of them; yet the line drifts through the mulga, light and unsubstantial as a shadow. They look neither to right nor left. They have an air of being wrapped in absorbing thought and of going about some business of their own in which man as a factor has faded out.

And it is so. For after months of wandering they are now on a pad they know well, for it leads to their old home camp where time and again they have found rest and freedom. Under the moon they are almost white. They fit so naturally into the landscape; they are so one with the spirit of the scene, that they might well have been contemporaries of Diprotodon and Genyornis, and it is strange to think that sixty years ago the land knew them not.

Suddenly, the mulga falls away and we emerge on to an open saltbush flat. A burst of moonlight turns it all to silver; and there, suddenly before us, is the conical mass of Undlepitcha, our landmark of the windy morning. We pass into its hot black shadow and out again into more mulga beyond, and when the dawn comes, the long purple line of the Everard is close at hand.

As we enter the hills and turn into the glen which leads to the camp, the silence is broken for the first time since we got under way. Old Snowy, the leader, begins to "talk;" a soft ululating call rising and falling with the swing of the stride, and very different from any other camel sound. It, passes from one to another down the line and it does not need the eager quickening of the pace to tell one what it means. A mile away, perched high on granite boulders, sharp against the sky-line, is a group of welcoming blacks, and below them is the splash of green that marks the water where we camp.

Home again; for man and beast.

13

THE CAR

CHIEF among the difficulties of collecting in the Centre, particularly of mammal collecting, are the hugeness of the area and the obscurity of the factors which determine the distribution of its fauna.

It is easy to select an area to work in, and usually not very difficult to get there; but there is a complete uncertainty of getting results on arrival; and the most carefully laid plans may have to give place at the eleventh hour to hasty improvisations involving weeks of travelling.

There are two ways in which these difficulties may be overcome: first and best, by having unlimited time, and second by having greatly increased mobility. Although camels are ideal when time stretches away from one as boundless as the terrain, they are apt to be a strain upon one's patience when it is limited to the three short months of a vacation, and for these reasons one's thoughts sometimes linger rather wistfully on the time-saving qualities of a motor car.

The car is now so universally in use in almost all parts of the Australian hinterland, that it is difficult for most of us to recall those not very distant years, when its intrusions into the bush were solely due to the adventurous "stunts" of record breakers from the cities; and odd to dwell on the aura of urban incongruity and ridicule which then invested it. In Central Australia, however, its success has been only partial. In the cattle country, where there is sufficient traffic to keep open tracks, its use is very general, and several long-distance mail-routes are maintained entirely by its aid. The trips from Maree to Birdsville, Farina to Innamincka, and the Alice to Birdum, for example, are regularly run by mail cars - frequently under conditions of such extraordinary difficulty as to leave one divided in wonderment, between the ruggedness of the modern machines and the pluck and resource of the men who drive them.

Still, rough as they are, these journeys are made over known routes where, even if the track has been wiped out by sand-drift or flood, the difficulties of the terrain are known as they are approached. It is quite otherwise when one attempts to move across country as freely as one would with camels or horses. True, long uninterrupted traverses are occasionally possible in virgin country by taking advantage of favourable conformations of surface; but one's free will is greatly curtailed, and deviations from these natural channels of least resistance lead one speedily into trouble.

In the Luritja Country the car is almost untried, except for the classical exploits of Michael Terry. His experience in this form of transport is so unique, however, that it is no safe guide as to what may be accomplished with ordinary equipment. It was with some misgivings, therefore, that the writer in 1934 undertook, with my brother, F.H.G. Finlayson, a small venture with a light 18 horse-power buckboard to test the performance of a standard car in this area.

South of the Musgrave-Mann-Tomkinson line of ranges, lies a great area of parallel east-to-west sand-ridges. Although an almost waterless region of somewhat forbidding character, it contains some of the chief mammal stations of the Centre, being ordinarily richer, both in species and numbers, than the more attractive country in and around the ranges. On a previous occasion I had time only to skirt its margins on the Officer, but with promising results. So, though it bade fair to be a very gruelling test for the car, and water-supply was uncertain, I was anxious to get deeper into it.

We left Ernabella in very hot weather, about the New Year, bound for Pundi - a little oasis in the sand-hills a hundred miles south-west. Travelling with camels, whose carrying capacity seems always to stretch magically to meet every emergency, rather spoils one for a light car, where every pound must be considered. In spite of determined efforts to keep the weight down, we still had over sixteen hundredweight on the springs, the biggest items being two forty-four-gallon drums of petrol and two seventeen-gallon canteens of water. In addition to ourselves, we now had with us two full-blood boys - Hector, a strapping man of thirty years or so, originally from the Everard, and Jerry, a youngster in his early teens, belonging to the sand-hill blacks.

Hector, though rather out of his latitude in the sand-hills, had made several trips to Pundi by camel, and was confident of his ability to hit off the waters. He was at fault once or twice and gave us some anxious moments when a leaky radiator was making inroads on the canteens, but he ultimately made good in each case. Both boys were highly delighted with the trip and took a keen and intelligent interest in the car and its handling. We drilled them systematically in lending a hand with repairs and adjustments. It was remarkable how quickly they fell into the routine of such proceedings and grasped the use of tools and the assembling of parts. Before the trip was over they could be trusted to jack up the car, take a rim off, prepare a tube for patching, fill radiator and tank, and do a dozen jobs with certainty, which greatly helped our progress.

The first afternoon's run was west, along the southern foot of the Musgraves to the waterhole called Erliwunyawunya. The going through this open park-like country is fairly good, though the loam proved unexpectedly heavy, having a rather spongy texture, like the intumescent clays of the Lake Eyre basin, known locally as "bull dust."

Coming into the place after dark we nearly blundered into a wide sandy creek-crossing at four miles per hour, but fortunately pulled up in time and backed out. We crossed it, as we crossed most subsequent ones, by posting the boys at strategic points in the sand so as to mark the best going, and then backing away a quarter-mile and charging it "flat out."

I was interested to see how their nerves would stand the ordeal of the approaching car. Although they had both seen cars before, we must have presented a rather terrifying spectacle as we bore down upon them out' of the dark, with the headlights streaming away over the flats and the exhaust bellowing like a banshee. I fully expected them to bolt into the timber before we hit the creek. They certainly wavered a little but stood their ground, and as we lurched over the top of the opposite slope they clambered aboard like old hands, and chattered excitedly over the episode all the way in to the water.

Next morning we were away at daylight and continued on down the range to Murranuckna, seventy-five miles from Ernabella. The going was still fairly good. We sighted several "mobs" of emus and lost much time in stalking them before I finally bagged one for the boys. The blacks are exceedingly fond of emu and are always disappointed if one passes a mob without a shot. Usually it pays to gratify them, as it keeps them in good humour and saves one's flour somewhat; but, when travelling, they always expect to carry the semi-cooked carcass about on the load until by a series of "snacks " - so to speak - they reduce the bird to a skeleton. During the process it exudes a rancid oil in quantity, and towards the end blankets the car in an aroma which we never seemed to have speed enough to escape. After this first experience, we usually found good excuses for shooting no more while travelling.

At Murranuckna we turned sharp south and leaving the range entered what is almost a new world-and one filled with tribulation for the motorist. Almost immediately we were in dense mulga which continued with occasional breaks to our next water at Pinindi, twenty-five miles south of the range.

Those who have read Terry's books on his truck expeditions farther north may have the impression that this crashing through the mulga is rather an exhilarating business. It may be so when one's chariot is rugged enough to relieve one of anxiety, but with a touring car it is one long nightmare of twisting and turning and backing and stalling and restarting, while one is deafened by the noise and half-blinded by the fine dust which arises, not from the soil so much, as from the foliage of the mulga.

The mulga in most of these belts is so dense that it was impossible to pick a track between the stems wide enough for the car; the only way to make progress was by pushing down the sticks which stood in the way. Having a good bumper-bar, we were able to do this pretty effectively with growing timber, but the dead trees, which are freely interspersed with the living and thickly litter the ground, were a more difficult problem. The sharp twigs and branchlets constantly threatened the radiator, while the tyres were menaced by the spiky roots of the upturned stumps. These last

THE BIRDSVILLE MAIL
Negotiating sand-hills near Ooroowillani.

ROUGH GOING IN THE PETERMANN GORGE

were especially venomous. They somewhat resemble those gruesome implements we used to read of in our early history books as being strewn on medieval battlefields to impede cavalry.

We were seldom out of second gear in these scrubs, and frequently in low. Boiling was almost continuous, and halts were necessary every few miles for cooling off, as the water consumption had to be watched very narrowly.

At about eleven miles from Murranuckna during one of these halts we discovered the first disaster-a badly staked radiator. This cost us half a day's delay. After trying in turn and discarding solder, spinifex gum, and shellac and sawdust as sealing media, we hit upon the most obvious - stiff dough, and with this homely material effected an excellent repair which held for the rest of the trip.

Hector now added to our troubles by developing an alarming vagueness as to the direction and distance of Pinindi. At midday of the third day out we rounded a granite rangelet which he said was that place. But as we could find no water there, and as the speedometer indicated that we were still seventeen miles short of the Pinindi of the maps, my faith in Hector as a guide received a shock. When questioned closely he admitted rather sheepishly that he was "sleued." Although this was disquieting so early in the piece, I could scarcely blame him as the noise and novelty of the car travelling must have been very upsetting to his navigation; further, both boys had frequently to devote all their energies to holding on. While I took some bearings on the peaks to the south and conned the map, I sent Hector out to look for water, and at the same time sort out his ideas and pick up some landmarks. He returned in two hours in high spirits, having found a small water high up in the granite and sighted a hill which he now declared to be the real Pinindi, on the course I had determined to follow. This we reached by sundown, after another six hours' tussle with the mulga, and were greatly relieved to find a good soak on the south side, and a fairly comfortable camp.

Next morning, steering south of west for Pundi, we topped .some rising ground at four miles and had a magnificent view of the country through which we had been struggling. The main range to the north was now only a faint blue outline; but rising from the plain to the west and south-west was a series of curiously shaped isolated peaks, some rugged and spinifex-clad right to their summits, like Pinindi, just left; others bare and smooth with great rock slides on their flanks, and all glinting a rich red in the morning sun.

Hector, who was now sure of his ground, could name but a few of the more prominent - Oolburra, Koonamutta, Ingya, Ungarra, Muckiri, and Kulpi - but the sand-hill Pitchenturras, who, by their aid, navigate the featureless country to the south, know and name everyone of them and recognize them instantly from the most diverse angles and view-points. These are almost the last of the granites. To the south of them, the sand has almost undisputed sway right down to the northern edge of the N ullarbor.

South of Pinindi the mulga falls away and we had a few miles of bumpy but open going over spinifex fiats. Our relief was short-lived however, since at 10 a.m. we struck the first of the sand-hills and thereafter were scarcely ever free from them. The ridges are not very alarming to casual inspection; their true devilishness from the motoring point of view only dawns upon one gradually. Few of them rise more than from sixty to seventy feet and they are anything from two hundred yards to half a mile apart, the interspaces being sandy fiats covered with spinifex and mallee and occasional kurrajongs. The difficulties they present are due to the fact that a direct frontal attack upon them can seldom succeed without a great deal of preparation, since many of the ridges are capped with an almost vertical crest. Even when this is demolished the going is so bumpy on the fiats that it is impossible to get up sufficient speed to carry one over. Fortunately, the height of the sand-hills is much less uniform than on the Diamantina, for example, where a single ridge may run unbroken for thirty miles. Here we were frequently able to find low vegetated gaps, though in doing so we added fifty per cent to our mileage. But very often no break could be seen, and a track had to be brushed across the crest and the hill taken by storm.

It took us twelve long hours to do the thirty-one miles to Pundi. The heat and glare of the sand, the roar of the exhaust, the incessant wrenching and jolting, and the wild scrambles up the hills to give a shove at the critical moment as she laboured on the crest, combined to make it the most exhausting day I can remember. Through it all, however, the blacks - clinging like ants to the bounding load - remained very cheerful and we had further cause to be thankful in a complete absence of mechanical or engine trouble.

Pundi is marked by a granite tor about sixty feet high, flanked by sheets of granite some acres in extent. At the north-east edge of these is a soak. A rain during the night, however, made us independent of this supply as we got thirty gallons of rain-water from pools on the slabs - a welcome find, for the soak water has a peculiar taste, and a smell which can only be described as aboriginal. The place is typical of many of the oases which serve the sand-hill Pitchenturras as rendezvous, in that generations of camping have destroyed the timber round about the water. This has led to an enhanced growth of small herbage, which gives the place a very verdant air. In spite of the wealth of vegetation, however, signs were not wanting that mammal life was much scarcer than on similar areas last year, and the time soon came when we could find no good excuse for postponing a resumption of the battle with the scrub.

The return journey across to the Officer and thence to Ernabella was largely a repetition of the outward one, with the difficulties due to mulga and tyre trouble greatly increased. We left Ernabella with six balloons in new condition and limped back without a single sound cover or tube. The alternation of sand-hills with scrubs makes the problem of tyre pressures a difficult one, since the sand is best negotiated with from eighteen to twenty pounds of air, while to avoid torn covers in the mulga one needs from thirty-five to thirty-eight pounds. Nothing short of extra heavy outsize truck balloons would stand up to such work for long.

Motorists who do most of their running on the bitumen may be interested in some figures of our mileages and petrol consumption. In planning the trip we had confidently reckoned on a minimum of fifty miles a day, and thought there might be days when that figure would be multiplied by two. Actually, our best day's run when breaking tracks over virgin country was forty-nine miles, while our average run for a ten hours' day was thirty miles. This is no more than one can do with pack-camels; with riding-camels it could be exceeded by one-third. With a load of sixteen hundred-weight and four passengers we averaged nine miles to the gallon of petrol, and by exercising the greatest care in cooling off at every opportunity, water consumption (a vital matter) was kept down to six gallons a day. Fully two-thirds of the mileage was done in second or low gear.

Once the tracks are broken, of course, a return upon them can be made with very much less trouble. Still, car travelling in such country in summer is not an attractive proposition. With camels, one can think and observe when on the move; the noise and movement of a car make both difficult, and every day ends in a headache and a condition bordering on exhaustion.

Two months later, when Pundi was only a painful memory, we were again in the car, homeward bound, purring down the well-used track that follows the old camel-pad from Ernabella to Oodnadatta, and ticking off the camel camps, one per hour - seven days in one.

Truly the car works miracles - but not in mulga and sand-hills.

14

THE WHITE MAN

ON the eastern fringes of the Luritja Country, six white men dwell.

From their frontier camps they look west over a vast territory where men form no permanent abodes; where even now Europeans venture but hazardously, and to its farther distances with no certainty of return. Presiding solitary over hundreds of square miles of territory, one thinks of them as much in terms of terrain as of personality, and their names come to mind, like the Greek chiefs before Troy, each indissolubly linked with that of the district over which its owner rules.

Their "stations" are almost upon the borders of the Aboriginal Reserves of Central and South Australia and will, therefore, mark the approximate limits of settlement in this part of the country, as long as the Reserves are inviolate. Tempe, the first to be established, is a cattle run with a history dating back to 1885. Its inception was chiefly due to the enterprise of the geologist, Dr Charles Chewings, who seems to have endowed his successors with an interest in science; thereby founding a tradition of helpfulness to investigation, which is fully maintained by B. Bowman, its present manager and part owner. It consists very largely of hill country and comprises the south-westerly portion of the James, the Levi, and George Gill ranges, and the early occupation of so remote a spot is due to the series of splendid waters, some at the foot of the ranges, some in gorges debouching upon well-grassed flats, the whole forming an ideal combination for the raising of cattle.

Almost from the first, however, it has been a storm centre in the clash of white man with black, since the western end of the George Gill, containing some of the best stock country, was a favourite gathering ground of the western bands, and the spearing of cattle rapidly became one of the chief attractions of the place to them. High up on the range may still be seen the sites of their beef feasts, for after spearing the cattle on the grassy flats, the beasts were dismembered and carried up to the top of the hills for cooking, so that the approach of a raiding police party could easily be observed. The number of cattle killed was considerable, but the indirect loss was still more serious, since the cattle, after one ambush, will no longer water in the gorges, and some of the choicest parts of the run were thus ungrazed.

The question is an ill one to argue with a cattleman, yet these killings were surely quite inevitable, and it is difficult to understand on what grounds the blacks could be expected to refrain from availing themselves of these "mountains of meat," which, to some extent, had displaced their own game. On the other hand, one can scarcely overestimate the pluck and energy of the men who worked the place year after year, usually alone so far as other whites were concerned, and with no more help than a handful of stock boys, frequently disaffected and in sympathy with the myalls.

There is some curious quality in the country which moulds a white man in a solitary habit. No matter what the occupation, an intense individualism develops; partnerships are few and generally short-lived; men live either quite alone or with black helpers only. Though they forgather occasionally for the interchange of news, an interval of six, even twelve, months between such contacts is not unusual. Half a dozen men constitute a big gathering, in which a restlessness soon develops, a sensation of being hemmed in by a great concourse of people, and after a few days they drift apart again, cordially, but thanking God inwardly, that the country still affords elbow-room between neighbours. The summer climate is such that few white women can endure it for long under the conditions of an outpost, so that the chief factor in the gregariousness of *homo* is permanently absent from the country.

Where waters are permanent, and good feed to be had, as on Tempe, horses, originally turned adrift, or escaped from station plants, have multiplied to a remarkable extent. Though descended from good station stock, these feral horses (brumbies as they are locally called) are mostly degenerate or undersized, and until recently they have been regarded as pests and were trapped or shot whenever opportunity offered. Since the price of horses rose suddenly in 1931, however, the pest has become an asset, for among the many "runts" there is a fair sprinkling of serviceable horses, which are now culled and marketed.

They are obtained either in the process of brumby running, in which the mob is galloped into a corral by a mounted party, or, more ingeniously, by a horse-trap. In summer the horses are frequent and regular drinkers and make well-beaten pads from the feeding-grounds to the waters of their choice. Around the most favourably-situated waterholes, heavy post and rail fences are built, in which a narrow gap is left, sufficient to admit one horse at a time. To each of the heavy posts which flank the gap, a sharpened six-foot sapling is bolted about breast high, so that the points project into the yard, and at the same time converge till they are about fourteen inches apart. The thirsty brumby enters the gap, squeezes between the springy saplings which open out to admit him to the yard, and then drinks his fill. When he attempts to quit, he is confronted by the sharp converging points, and after a half-hearted attempt to force a passage, during which he gets pricked, he retires to wander disconsolately round the fence till someone calls for him.

Much more recent than the cattle on Tempe, and on W. Mac-namara's country to the north of it, are the sheep ventures which were the chief factors in establishing the posts to the south. W. H. Liddle pioneered their introduction into the south-west Centre, by taking up a block of virgin mulga country between the Basedow and Wollara ranges and depasturing thereon a thousand merino cross-breds, which he travelled up from Oodnadatta, two hundred and seventy miles away. He was closely followed by Pearce at the running water of Murrachurra, fifty miles south; and somewhat later by Fergusson, in the grass country enclosed by the Musgraves at Ernabella.

The keeping of sheep in such conditions as exist in this virgin country constituted a radical departure in procedure, and one for which a speedy failure was confidently predicted. The economic outcome is still uncertain, but chiefly owing to the remoteness of markets and the crushing freight charges, since the sheep themselves have thriven remarkably.

To appreciate fully the indomitable pluck and resource which have directed these experiments it must be remembered that since large areas are essential for success, fencing on any scale is quite out of the question owing to the enormous expense involved; and as the country is infested with wild dogs, the flocks must be shepherded the long day through and brought in every night and yarded. All this has been possible only through the co-operation of the blacks. Small groups have attached themselves, more or less permanently, to each of the settlers. The gins act as shepherdesses while the men follow a hunting life, the rigours of which are now much reduced, owing to the white man's "tucker," which comes regularly to hand.

It is an extraordinarily incongruous association; almost literally the cattle wolf lying down with the lamb. But it is significant that the bitter experiences of the cattle runs have not so far been repeated in these new ventures; partly, no doubt, because the blacks have been greatly reduced; but partly, too, because regular feeding of those employed has led to a genuine co-operation, and a much better feeling between the parties.

Killings are almost unknown, and now that the gins have seen several shearings, they understand something of the value of their charges and their shepherding leaves little to be desired. But at first it was casual in the extreme, owing, probably, to a difficulty in understanding why one man should need all that meat. In those first days a count in at night might be twenty short. Twenty sheep gone in one day from a flock of a thousand in a year of three hundred and sixty-five days, makes for some uneasy exercises in mental arithmetic on the part of a sheep-man.

Not the least of his exasperations at such times was the difficulty in obtaining precise information as to the direction taken by the strays. There is, to our seeming, a peculiar vagueness in the Luritja method of

A WORKING CAMP
Embalming a maala at Pundi.

OUTWARD BOUND
Leaving the Finke River for the western country.

indicating direction. In response to anxious and pressing questions as to the whereabouts of the truants, the gins, slightly embarrassed, stand on one foot and, meditatively scratching themselves with the other, remark, "Sheepee go thataway," "whichaway" being indicated by a fluttering gesture of the hand, embracing half the horizon. Not very soothing to a man eager to get a fresh tracking party out, but insistence is useless.

The exigencies of food and water prevent the formation of permanent homesteads. The flock must be travelled out to feed and back to camp each day, and this concentration on small areas leads to the feed rapidly being eaten out. Then, too, many of the waters relied on are transient affairs with a life of only a few weeks, and as the water is used up a move must be made to another which in the meantime has been located by scouts. Life thus becomes an affair of shifting camps and in many curious ways is lived quite in the style of the more rural of the Biblical patriarchs.

The moving of the establishment to pastures new is a gala day with the blacks, for they have no love for "sitting down" in one place for long, and their nomad spirits rise gleefully to such occasions.

First, with skylarking and shrill laughter, go the younger gins and older children, driving the sheep ahead of them, and with the milch goats forming a far flung fringe to the flock, as befits their enterprising nature. Then follow the older folk and young children, with the horses and donkeys and a long string of camels with all the heavy camp gear and the household goods. Next are the lordly bucks who own the shepherdesses as their wives or daughters. They walk easily, each with but a handful of spears, for it is their women who do the white man's work, and burdens are not for such as they. And last, bringing up the rear on a stocky pony, and shouting stentorian directions to the giggling gins, comes the solitary, bearded white man.

A curious scene. As the procession passes, with its babel of sounds and animal smells, time seems to have slipped back some thousands of years and it is the wealth of a shepherd king of old that files before one.

The six pioneers of the fringe are chiefly devoted to pastoral pursuits. Although they cannot be said to be stationary, yet at least their wanderings are confined to more or less restricted areas. It is quite other with the fluctuating population of white nomads who make the six camps their last ports of call, as it were, on their camel voyages into the country further west. They are men of a certain physical uniformity, but with a wide range in the scale of mental and moral worth. In an environment and under a mode of life, where the only effective restraints upon a white man are self imposed, men tend either to develop a strength of character and rectitude of a high order, or to slump altogether into blackguardism. One gladly admits a plentiful representation of the first type. But the candid chronicler of affairs in the Centre to-day cannot do other than draw attention to the existence of a debased element whose presence is the most serious obstacle to the correct adjustment of the two races. They are a menace also to those who make the charitable assumption that the traditional standards of honesty and fair dealing amongst bushmen are universal.

The lowest of these creatures are comparatively recent derivations from the criminal underworld of the cities, and it is a bitter thought that scores of natives, even on the Reserve itself, have received their first impressions of the white race from men in whom foulness and treachery were perfectly blended. The eradication of this pest by the adequate policing of the country is one of the most pressing needs of the territory.

Very different are the men of the other category - products of a discipline whose rigours have left them with something of the largeness and simplicity of the country itself. To these, many interests call; but prospecting is perhaps the chief.

Sudden wealth beckons most men with the same appeal, and in the Centre all men are, or have been, or will become, prospectors. Mines and mining are in the air. From the bar-tenders at the "pubs" on the line, to the farthest wanderer in the west, all men have felt the fever of gold and opal; and most will talk overpoweringly a jargon bristling with "lodes" and "dykes," "reefs" and "colours," and the astonishing results of yet more astonishing assays.

Usually it is a passing, or at least an intermittent madness. There are those, however, who never recover, and they become the *elite* of the profession, the high priests of the cult. As the obsession grows, they lose all contact with the race of men, and brood alone in the outer solitudes. But it is no soft life of the anchorite they live. In pursuit of an idea, in testing a theory, they spend their days in orgies of labour, and single-handed with shovel and pick, rear many a monument in the wilderness to their faith in empiricism. By ordinary men they are regarded with a certain reverence, and all the dicta of science will not prevail against their opinion. They are steeped in strange chemistries, not of the Schools; and by night, the issues of the day's work are decided by the simple arbitrament of "acid," borax and fire.

Perhaps you are a stranger within the gates. Having eaten, you explain yourself and your mission. He expresses a naive incredulity that anyone should be really interested in rats;" then, in reminiscent mood, he tells you of the several rare and highly curious species he has been fortunate enough to see at various times and places. These times and places are usually remote, and long before the narrative is done, you perceive that his friendly desire to appear interested in your work, has led him to raise the plane of the discussion from fact to fancy.

You do not make the mistake of doubting him, however; but later you disclose some slight knowledge of the metals and mineralogy, and warming to the work, you build up for his eager ear, a complete theory of the occurrence of ore bodies, based on radio-active and other less well-known transformations. This discourse also, would create considerable astonishment in scientific circles; but under the circumstances a devotion to orthodoxy is of less moment than a free interchange of courtesies. As the night wears on, you draw closer together over the fire; the unwonted exercise of speech breaks down the barriers of caution. At length he tells you of that which gives a meaning to his existence. It is the "Lost Reef." And though you have heard that story up and down the country, till it has become a weariness, yet as you mark his fanatic earnestness, you half believe it yourself.

Hope dies hard; and the credulity of the investing public seems boundless. But the sober judgment of geologists and mining men holds out little prospect of valuable mineral finds in much of the country in which prospectors seek their fortune.

More profitable is "dogging." The indigenous mammals of the area have little commercial value in themselves, and there is nothing approaching a fur-trade or even one of hides. Nevertheless, a traffic has grown up of late years, almost deserving to be called an industry, which is centred in the dingo, or wild dog of the country. Although a mild tempered dog so far as man is concerned, and in virgin country a mixed feeder, depending partly on fruits (especially those of the numerous Solanums) the dingo nevertheless easily becomes a wanton and confirmed killer of sheep and calves, and, in all parts of the country, a scourge to pastoral enterprise. In the coastal belts and in other long-settled districts, the wild dog has been extirpated or reduced to vanishing point; but in the unoccupied parts of the Centre he occurs in very large numbers, owing partly to the extension and multiplication of the rabbit providing a greatly increased food-supply. These parts act as potential reservoirs from which (as some consider) the pest constantly overflows into the pastoral country.

The aggregate damage done by dogs is very great, and paternal Governments now come to the rescue by paying a bonus for every dog killed. The price paid varies in different districts from £2 to 7s. 6d., but most of the dogs taken are worth from 7s. 6d. to 10s. each, and some idea of the earnings made in the business may be gained from the fact that within recent years, three partners, working separately during a season of four to five months, obtained over three thousand scalps. Payment for scalps was begun in South Australia in 1913 and in Central Australia and Western Australia, in 1924. Since then the total number of scalps obtained in these States is 510,500, involving a disbursement in rewards of approximately £344,000.

In the Central areas, although a proportion of these huge tallies is got directly by shooting and trapping and poisoning, the great bulk is obtained by trading with the blacks, whose minute knowledge of the habits of the dogs, and particularly of their seasonal movements and breeding places, enables them to get results quite beyond the reach of a white man alone. Unlike most of the marsupials of the Centre, which to a great extent are independent of surface waters, the dingo is a frequent drinker, and in summer tends to concentrate about the ranges, where most of the permanent waters are to be found. On the other hand, in the cool weather when they need water less frequently, the open sand country is preferred, because of its greater attractions as a hunting-ground. Here in the early winter the sluts litter so that a plentiful food-supply simplifies the rearing of the pups.

The pups are the chief factor in the success of a dogging venture. Every pup is a potential killer and until recently the same bonus was paid for a suckling as for a seasoned old warrigal. The blacks, of course, are not slow to realize this, and as the labour of tracking up and spearing a single adult dog is as great as, or greater than, that in-volved in locating a litter, they do not molest the breeding sluts, but when the time is ripe, descend upon the family and secure a haul of six or eight instead of one.

The token, on which payment of the bonus is made, is a scalp, and over the Luritja Country scalps have now become a sort of currency, filling the same place in the intercourse of the two peoples as the beaver skin formerly did in the territories of the Hudson's Bay Company.

The scalping habit has taken firm root amongst the blacks and is sometimes a sad embarrassment to mammal collecting. West of the Rawlinson and south of the Everard, there occurs in the sand country a little-known race of the marsupial anteater, *Myrmecobius fasciatus.* The desert form is a very beautiful little animal, the most brilliantly coloured of all the Australian mammals, having a glossy coat of a rich, almost orange-scarlet colour, crossed by a series of transverse white bands. When the importance of getting specimens of the animal was urged upon a party of good dog-hunters, they readily agreed to try. Some days later they returned to camp with the glad news that they had secured ten. But when they proudly produced the evidence of their success, a stricken silence fell. They had brought back ten scalps only.

The growth of a systematic aviculture throughout the world has given rise to another minor industry of inland Australia; that of the bird-netter. Until comparatively recently this had its headquarters in the north-west where some of the most brilliantly coloured of the finches occur in enormous numbers. But since the sudden reappearance in 1930 of the supposedly extinct scarlet-chested parrot, *Neophema splendida,* the south-western Centre has had more attraction for the "birder," and several men are now engaged in its quest, and in that of the equally beautiful Alexandra parrakeet, and of Bourke's parrot, and the exquisite little budgerigar.

The reappearance of *splendida* proved to be as transient as it was unexpected, and the species seems to be fading again into the unknown from which it came; but while it graced the country with its presence, it offered a prize worth trying for. Twenty-five pounds was the price paid for the first pair sent down to Adelaide. To-day, £100, it is stated, would be paid for a pair on the London market.

Dogging, birding, prospecting: these are the ostensible reasons why men head their camels west of the settlements.

But the material rewards are often the least of the attractions of such undertakings, and the real motive which drives men on is the wanderlust which all wide, empty lands stir in men of vigour. Here, in the Centre, it may be indulged on a vast scale, and as feats of bushcraft and judgment, some of these. journeys of doggers and prospectors into unmapped country, deserve a more permanent record than the network of camel pads which they have left on the sand. Many a well-equipped surveying or exploring party breaking into what was thought to be virgin country, has been startled by such evidence of unofficial forerunners.

Some of the most risky of these feats have been achieved by solitary white men travelling with three or four camels and with the scantiest of equipment. They were gambles with death, yet the survivors, when they can be induced to speak of them at all, do so lightly and with an easy jest. In the idiom of the country, quaint and forceful as speech tends to be where the issues of life are simple, the verb "to die" is unknown and is replaced by "to perish." Not, however, with any melodramatic intent, but so as to convey an implication of grim jest. "To perish," is to die by weathering, and like gutta-percha, men lose elasticity in the change, and the end product is known far and wide as a "stiff un."

To watch a string leave camp on a long trip west, or another return after months of absence is a never-failing interest; the more so if one's own lot is cast with the venture. For all that the scene is set in red sand, under an ardent sun, and with a beast of Asia as its chief *motif*, there is little of the Orient ill; the spirit which prompts men to these lonely tilts with fortune. As the line forges ahead over the gently undulating terrain, the long, swinging motion brings constantly to mind a comparison with seas and seafaring. And for this there are other sanctions, for these land-farings do but continue a tradition begun under grey skies upon an iron coast. And in the hiss of cushioned feet in the hot sand, one may catch again the whisper of a high prow, as a long-ship takes the swell.

The Norse blood stirs within us yet.

MAP
OF THE
South Western portion of
CENTRAL AUSTRALIA

Compiled from existing maps of the
early Explorers, of Official Surveys, and of
Chewings, Madigan, Terry and Mackay, by

H. H. Finlayson

with additional data along the
Author's Travelling Routes.

1931 — 1935.

── *REFERENCE* ──

Railways ....
State Boundaries ....
Approx. western limit of Stock (1935) ? ...
Author's Travelling Routes ....
Water Holes (in streams beds etc.) .... W.Hs.
Rock WaterHoles .... R.Hs.
Soakages .... Sks.
Homesteads .... H.S.

── SCALE OF MILES ──

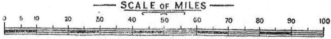

0 5 10   20   30   40   50   60   70   80   90 100

H E POWELL, GOVERNMENT PHOTOLITHOGRAPHER, ADELAIDE

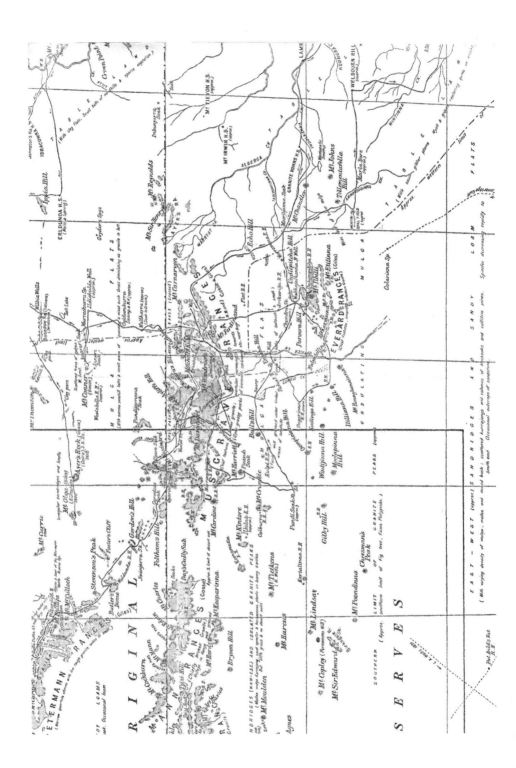

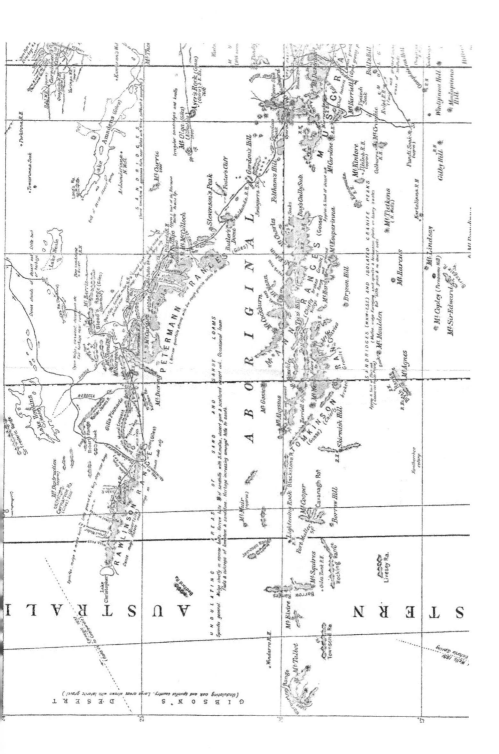

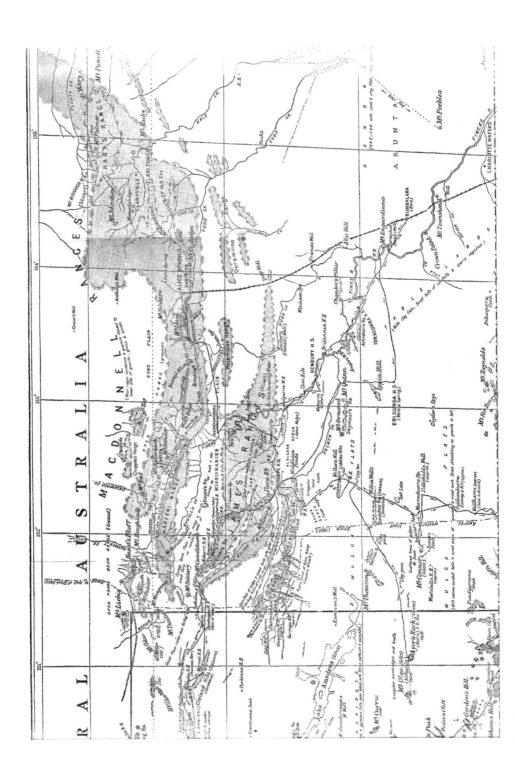

132

9 781922 698803

Printed by BoD™in Norderstedt, Germany